Allied Artillery
of
World War Two

Allied Artillery
of
World War Two

Ian V. Hogg

The Crowood Press

First published in 1998 by
The Crowood Press Ltd
Ramsbury, Marlborough
Wiltshire SN8 2HR

British Library Cataloguing-in-Publication Data
A catalogue record for this book is available from the British Library.

ISBN 1 86126 165 9

Typeset by Textype Typesetters, Cambridge

Printed and bound in Great Britain by the Bath Press

To my wife, Anna Teresa, who has frequently marched around Aberdeen Proving Ground,
and other military boneyards, taking pictures of guns, tanks,
missiles and other fauna, without once asking why.
Here are some of the fruits of your labours.

Contents

1 Introduction: Setting the Scene

In 1919, the artillerymen of the armies which had fought in the 1914–18 conflict might well have contemplated Kipling's line: 'They have taught us no end of a lesson . . .'

THE END OF THE FIRST WORLD WAR

Artillery had entered the war in 1914 as a small auxiliary to the field army, supported by an even smaller 'siege train'. They had ended it as a major component of every army – it has been estimated that, at one stage of the war, one-third of all the troops embroiled in the fighting were gunners – armed with a colossal armoury of artillery of types not even contemplated four short years before. They had begun the war, in many cases, by firing over open sights at charging cavalry, in the best traditions of the Peninsular War, and ended it using aerial observation, predicted fire, fire-plans of immense complexity, meteorological corrections, and self-propelled guns on tracked mountings. With the end of the First World War, it was time to take stock and analyse what had been learned.

One of the first steps was to scrap a vast number of guns, principally those of pre-war origin, which had, of necessity, remained in service even though they were obsolete. In addition, large numbers of guns were sold off or donated to those Middle European countries that had emerged from the war as independent states, including Poland, Czechoslovakia, Latvia, Estonia, Lithuania and the Balkans. The abrupt cancellation of wartime contracts also killed off a number of guns in the process of development, such as the British 3.6in AA gun and the American 4.7in AA gun, as well as curtailing the manufacture of many guns which represented the current generation of artillery.

This purge was followed by financial retrenchment. The 'War to End All Wars' had been fought and won, the butcher's bill was still being argued over, and the demand for disarmament was heard in all corners. Any national finances that had survived the war were in demand for social reforms, housing and pensions, and other spending promises that had been made by the politicians during the war, which now had to be honoured. The first target for financial retrenchment was obvious: the armed forces.

ARTILLERY RE-DEVELOPMENT

Throughout the 1920s, the artillerymen of the world discussed, analysed, planned, designed and argued, but precious little equipment or re-organization appeared as a result of all their work, since this would cost money. At this time, the commandant of the British Army's tank school was given the sum of fifty pounds to cover one year's development of a new tank machine gun; even allowing for the purchasing power of the pound in the 1920s, such a sum was unlikely to uncover any radical advance in technology.

Even so, enough money was scraped up here and there for some experiments, including the British development of an 18-pounder self-propelled gun (the 'Birch' gun, named after Sir Noel Birch, Master-General of the Ordnance). By 1927, a handful of these were provided for an 'Armoured Experimental Force', and they proved to be versatile and efficient weapons. The gun was mounted on the chassis and hull of the Vickers medium tank and could act as an anti-tank gun, a close infantry support gun, or a conventional field gun, as required; it was even provided with receiver dials, which could be connected to an anti-aircraft predictor, converting it into an AA gun (with a maximum elevation of 90 degrees).

However, the 1920s was a time of bitter schism between the conservative and radical groups within the army; generally, the conservatives wanted to adapt modern equipment to a conventional organization of forces, while the radicals were convinced that a complete re-alignment of the army around the tank was the only way ahead. They saw no need for a self-propelled gun where a suitably armed tank could do the same job, or, if they had to have a self-propelled gun, they preferred to form a 'Royal Tank Artillery' to operate it. Needless to say, this idea did not go down well with the Royal Regiment of Artillery, and somewhere along the line – the truth has never been uncovered and never will be – the Birch gun was removed from the establishments and scrapped.

With the demise of the SP gun, the next question was the future of the 18-pounder and the 4.5in howitzer, and then how to replace the AA artillery, the 3in 20-cwt gun, with something more powerful. A dedicated anti-tank gun was also being investigated; what would it be and who would operate it? While all this was going on, there was also the vexed question of the defence of the new naval base at Singapore, an on–off saga depending upon the political whim of the moment, and bedevilled by the 1922 Washington Conference on Naval Limitation. *Inter alia*, this laid down restrictive clauses, forbidding the construction of new fortifications or defences in the Pacific Ocean area, so that Hong Kong's re-armament became questionable.

DIFFERENT TACTICS

The split between the conservatives and the radicals also extended to tactics. In general terms, the conservatives maintained that the trench warfare of 1914–18 had been an aberrant form of warfare, that the more conventional mobile warfare would be seen in the future, and that the army's prime task, therefore, was to close with the enemy's main force and destroy it. For this, the conventional mix of infantry, artillery and cavalry – with the tanks playing the cavalry role – was the correct one.

The radicals preferred the idea of avoiding headlong clashes and the resultant casualties, and wanted to aim for lightning surgical strikes at the enemy's lines of communication and supply, its headquarters, and its supply dumps. With the severing of these lines, the 'nerves' of a force would be severed; if the headquarters was crushed, the 'brain' of the force was crushed. With no brain and no nerves, the individual units would wither and die, as a tree dies if its roots are destroyed and its trunk cut. Such a surgical manoeuvre would be carried out by tanks – lots and lots of them. With so many tanks, there would be no need for much infantry or artillery.

These radical theories may have been right, but lots and lots of tanks meant lots and lots of money, and upon that rock the radical ship foundered, the conservatives winning by default. The only army that could be afforded was one built along conventional lines, and the proposal for an all-conquering all-armoured army did not have a chance.

With this hurdle cleared, the artillerymen now saw that their prime task was to look at the technology and techniques that the First World War had produced, and adapt them to mobile forms of warfare. It was one thing to produce a complex barrage plan when the guns were in the same places that they had occupied for the past six months, and were certain to remain in them for the duration of the forthcoming battle; time was of little object and the plan could be carefully plotted and worked out, with data provided for every gun involved. However, in a fluid war, the guns might not be in place for twenty-four hours before being ordered to perform some fire plan, and in another twenty-four hours the opportunity would be lost. Ponderous 'siege warfare' techniques needed to be stream-lined and simplified, so that results could be achieved in far less time and with far less manpower.

COMMUNICATION

The final, and perhaps the most important, problem to be faced was that of communication. The First World War was unique in one respect, in that it was a war in which the commanders lost touch with the commanded as soon as the battle began. Prior to 1914, warfare had been a matter of individual battles, small enough to allow a commander to oversee what was going on and, with a staff of messengers and perhaps flag signalling, to control what was happening. However, in 1915–18, once the infantry had gone 'over the top' and begun advancing towards the enemy, they were virtually incommunicado. There was no radio; telephones could not be strung fast enough, and, even if they were, the lines would be cut within minutes by shellfire; runners attempting to go back with information or forward with orders were invariably killed or wounded, or could not find their destination in the fog of war, and the mud and shelled landscape. As a result, artillery fire was pre-ordained; so-and-so would happen at such-and-such a time, based upon the assumption that, by that time, some phase of the infantry's attack would have been successfully completed. If, as generally happened, the infantry was held up, the artillery fire was duly delivered, to no effect, and with the foot soldiers receiving no benefit from it. If the infantry got ahead of their plans, there was the added danger that the artillery's protective fire might well land among them.

Communication between the infantry and the supporting artillery was vital, as was lateral communication between the artillery units themselves. The obvious solution to the problem was radio, but the 'wireless', as it was then known, was a somewhat delicate device in the 1920s. It was principally used by armed forces for wireless telegraphy – the sending of messages by Morse code. Speech radio as it is known today began to appear in 1918, after the invention of the thermionic valve, but it was some time before reliable and robust radio sets, capable of being operated by the simple soldier, were perfected.

THE EARLY 1930s

An eminent French politician, at the signing of the peace treaty in Paris in 1919, commented, 'This is not peace, this is a twenty-year armistice.' By the early 1930s, the indications were that his estimate might be close to the truth. The pace of military thinking quickened. Final assessments of possible gun designs were appraised and choices made; theoretical organizations and techniques were tried on a small scale, modified, approved and adopted. Mechanization of armies – in the widest sense, not just tanks, but trucks and cars as well – was pushed forward. Radio was perfected, its operation practised, and its impact upon command and control tested. One by one, the various blocks that go to build an integrated artillery force were checked and put in place.

This was happening not only in Britain. In the USA, the process was much the same, although slower and less intense, since the army had been ruthlessly cut back in the immediate post-war years. The US army had ample wartime equipment remaining, as did the British army; many wartime contracts for manufacture of artillery had been allowed to complete, if not to their original quantities, at least to quantities sufficient to provide the army with more than it immediately required.

THE WESTERVELT REPORT

One important step in 1918–19 was the assembly of the Caliber Board, more frequently called the Westervelt Board, after its president, General William I. Westervelt (later to be Chief of Staff).

11

Early days of mechanization: a British 6in howitzer and tracked ammunition trailer being towed by a tractor in India in the early 1930s. The tractor appears to be somewhat under-powered

The board was charged with conducting a wide-ranging enquiry into the weapons used by the Allies during the war, and making recommendations as to which weapons should be perpetuated, which discarded, and what new weapons should be developed. The board reported in 1919 and decreed that the standard field artillery piece should be a 105mm howitzer, that the contemporary 75mm gun should be relegated to a minor position, and that various other weapons should be developed or improved.

Since a wholesale re-armament was out of the question, the army set about a detailed examination of the guns they intended to keep, in order to see how they could be improved. A research and design programme began, and managed, by the late 1930s, at low priority and without very much money, to produce sound designs for everything the Westervelt board had recommended. Not only had these guns been designed, they had also been carefully re-designed by production engineers, with drawings being prepared, so that production could commence at any time. The only delay would be the organization of the factories and the recruitment of

a workforce.

Mechanization had also been put in train (although the US Army was still relying upon horse cavalry for its scouting until 1940) which, as with other countries, had meant a hurried re-drawing of some gun designs, to equip them with pneumatic tyres and suitable connections for towing behind trucks. The American arguments for and against tanks were similar to those in other countries, but much less intense; an Act of Congress in 1921 had specifically directed that tanks were infantry equipment, and this meant that the argument did not impinge upon the artillery.

Anti-aircraft artillery had also featured in the Westervelt report, and its recommendations were taken up with alacrity, not only with regard to gun design but also in the matter of fire control. The idea of an electro-mechanical computer (called a 'director' in this application) was addressed quite early in the 1920s, with the Sperry Gyroscope company being approached for its ideas. Once the gun received the data, the next stage of development was to fire the shells in the right direction. By 1931, the experimental staff at

Aberdeen Proving Ground in Maryland were demonstrating a 4in AA gun with full remote power control. All the gunners had to do was load and fire it as fast as possible, the azimuth and elevation being set electrically by signals sent from the remote command post. It was not particularly accurate – no first prototype ever is – but it represented, none the less, a remarkable mechanical achievement. It was another twelve years before it was accurate and reliable enough to become part of a service equipment.

The inventory of equipment held by the US Army, in service and in reserve, in June 1940 makes interesting reading. The anti-aircraft branch had eight 37mm guns, 807 3in and thirteen 105mm guns. The anti-tank branch had 228 37mm guns. The field artillery had 4,236 75mm guns of several different patterns, ninety-one 75mm howitzers, fourteen 105mm howitzers, 973 155mm guns, 2,791 155mm howitzers, of which 598 had been adapted for high-speed towing, 475 8in howitzers (ex-British) and 320 240mm howitzers. The greater part of this list was lying in stores covered in grease and had not been disturbed since 1919. Apart from the fourteen 105mm howitzers, the ninety-one 75mm howitzers and a handful of 155mm guns, the remainder were obsolete. (The army also had nowhere near the number of men necessary to man all these weapons.) However, behind the scenes, the design offices and manufacturing plants were gearing up for the production of completely fresh designs in all categories.

COAST DEFENCE

American coast defence artillery was governed by the decisions of two boards of enquiry. The Endicott Board of 1888 and the Taft Board of 1903 were milestones in history, and their decisions were still being quoted in the 1920s as the arbiter for the armament of a particular fort. Such remarks as 'the report of the Endicott Board, as modified by the report of the Taft Board, requires the provision of eight 12 inch guns in this work; 6 have been provided, 2 more remain to be provided' appeared in the annual reports of the Chief of Ordnance, and were considered valid justification for armament demands.

The Washington Conference in the 1920s brought many changes, and caused the British and the Americans a few headaches; for the Americans, it forbade any improvement of the defences of the Philippines and other outlying dependencies. Fortunately, these defences had been completed as recently as 1915, so immediate upgrading was not vital. However, the naval armament restrictions agreed by the conference meant that the US Navy found itself with a quantity of surplus 16in guns; it decided to offer them to the Army for coast defence. This solution was marred by the fact that coast defence mountings would have to be made – they would be expensive, and there was insufficient money available. Having plenty of guns, but no means of mounting them and nowhere to mount them, must have been frustrating, but this particular impasse was overcome.

RUSSIA

Russia was a special case, quite different from the other Allies. The Russians had elected out of the war in 1917, and occupied themselves with a bloody civil war until 1921–22. Moreover, Russia's artillery manufacturing capacity was limited; in pre-1914 days, most of its guns and howitzers – certainly the better ones – came from Krupp of Germany and Schneider of France, sometimes being built under licence in the Putilov or Obuchov gun factories. After 1917, no supplies came from abroad, and the output of the two factories was sporadic at best. By the middle 1920s, the condition of the artillery branch of the Red Army was poor, their guns being almost obsolete in design, as well as being worn out.

One of the features of the between-wars years was the periodic announcement by the Soviets of a 'Five-Year Plan'; the first of these, ordered by Stalin in 1928, announced his intention to build up the heavy engineering industry so that agricultural machinery could be manufactured rather than imported. The second plan, in 1933, provided for the manufacture of the agricultural machinery. However, for every factory making agricultural machinery there were two making tanks or artillery; these Five-Year Plans were camouflage for heavy armament construction plants. As a result, by the early 1930s, artillery was coming forward in large quantities. Initially, the old Tsarist models were put back into production, but very quickly these designs were overhauled in the light of modern technology and production began again. By the time a sufficiency of these modernized weapons was on hand, the designers had produced drawings for new equipments. Production of these began in about 1935–36, in time to provide ample artillery for the 1939–40 'Winter War', and for the 1941 invasion by Germany.

As is frequently the case with Soviet history, reliable, truthful and complete information on artillery doctrines, techniques and equipment is hard to come by. It is not possible to give a complete description or analysis, but one or two features stand out.

First, the Red Army's attitude to the employment of artillery was different from that of the Western allies. Irrespective of its tactical employment, title or 'job description', every Soviet gun that could be depressed to point-blank was an anti-tank gun as soon as a tank appeared within its sight. As a result of this policy, every gun short of the really heavy artillery was issued with an anti-tank projectile.

In the positioning of guns, the immediate support of local units was the primary factor. The Western concept of command of artillery being exercised at the highest possible level, with orders being passed down the chain, did not apply; there was a higher command, but the absence of sophisticated radio networks precluded anything other than administrative command being exercised. Tactical command devolved upon, at the highest, a divisional artillery officer. An exception to this was the occasional formation of an 'Artillery Corps' or even an 'Artillery Army'. These were unlike any other army or corps in the world, being composed entirely of artillery regiments, and they were wielded as a massive reinforcement for set-piece battles. This sort of formation allowed such concentrations as the 32,143 guns and mortars that supported the Soviet attack across the Vistula river in January 1945.

This system was used because the only way to concentrate the fire of thousands of guns was to collect them together as tightly as possible under one hand; it was the communications problem once more. The Soviet set-up did not permit the use of dispersed artillery formations linked by radio and commanded on to a single target as easily as the British and American set-ups did. The gradual adoption of this system was achieved by a whittling down of the divisional artillery strengths; by 1945, the artillery of the average infantry division numbered no more than about forty guns of all types and sizes, most of which were direct-fire infantry-accompanying weapons. The remaining guns had all been moved across to the next higher artillery formations.

TECHNOLOGY

The technical features of individual guns are discussed where relevant in the book; one or two features of technology were, however, common to many guns of many makers, and began to be used regularly during the Second World War. Among the most important of these was the autofrettaged (or self-hooped, or cold-worked) gun barrel. During the First World War, guns were 'built up' or 'wire-wound', the two techniques being cross-linked.

In a built-up gun, the barrel – the rifled tube – is relatively thin, and is surrounded by a succession of larger tubes, each heated and then shrunk on to the previous one, until the complete gun body is made up of a number of tubes, the number varying at different points on the barrel. The chamber area, subject to the greatest pressure, has more layers than the 'chase', the section of the gun in front of the trunnions and ending in the muzzle.

A wire-wound gun is similar in general construction, but the place of one of the tubes is taken by miles and miles of high-tensile steel ribbon wound in several tight layers around the tube beneath – usually the actual barrel. This is then held in place by another tube heated and shrunk over it, and, sometimes, more tubes over the chamber.

Both types of construction were designed to place the barrel in a state of compression, so that the pressure of the explosive force inside when the gun fired was safely contained, and the barrel was prevented from expanding. Both involved precise and heavy machining, careful fitting and slow construction. A 15in naval gun could take almost a year to manufacture.

During the First World War, British and French scientists developed an entirely new method of constructing a gun barrel from one piece of steel. The barrel was bored out and shaped internally, below its intended dimensions. It was then tightly plugged at both ends and oil was pumped into the interior of the barrel at very high pressure. This pressure expanded the inner layers of steel beyond their elastic limit, so that, when the pressure was released and the oil drained off, the interior was expanded to the correct dimensions. The outer layers, however, had not expanded, so that, in effect, they were compressing the inner layers and doing the same job as the wire, or the additional tubes (properly called 'hoops') of the built-up barrel. As a result of this development, the manufacture of gun barrels became a much faster business, and also used less steel. Virtually every land service artillery gun manufactured in Britain, France and the USA after 1930 followed this autofrettaged pattern.

The second technical innovation was the gradual adoption of the muzzle brake. This is a device fitted to the gun muzzle, with holes or slots on its sides. As the shell passes through the brake, some of the propelling gas escapes through these holes or slots and is directed sideways and slightly rearwards. As a result, the gas exerts a forward thrust against the sides of the holes or slots, to try and push the brake, and hence the gun barrel, forward, in opposition to the normal recoil force that is pushing it back.

A well-designed brake can reduce the recoil force by a considerable amount. The gun can either be given a more powerful propelling charge and fired safely, without wrecking the recoil system, or the recoil system itself can be made lighter. It has been demonstrated that a muzzle brake can be designed to absorb as much as 65 per cent of the recoil force; unfortunately, it is necessary to divert the gas well to the rear rather than simply to the side, which makes life unpleasant and even dangerous for the gun detachment. However, a 30 per cent efficiency is generally possible without endangering the gunners.

Not every gun has a muzzle brake, since not every gun needs one. Anti-tank guns, where lightness counts, use one so as to save weight in the recoil system and carriage and yet still fire as heavy a charge as possible. Anti-aircraft guns do not usually have one, since weight is less of a limiting factor. Soviet field guns usually had them, because the Soviet designers tended to work to a lower factor of safety than British designers; consequently, their guns are a good deal lighter than a comparable British or American gun. Adding a muzzle brake reduced the stress on the carriage and made this lightness acceptable.

AMMUNITION

Generally, the British and American artilleries ended the war using the guns with which they had begun it. Mostly of 1930s design, these guns needed no serious modification to improve their performance. However, modifications to the ammunition were explored by all the combatants during the war.

In the early part of the war, most of the effort was directed towards cheaper and simpler ammunition production, resulting in some frightening experiments with cast-iron shells, substitute explosives, steel cartridge cases and similar expedients. These were gradually abandoned once it was realized that such extreme policies were not necessary (although

American troops at peacetime practice with the 75mm M1897A4 gun, their standard field weapon

both the Americans and the Germans made highly successful steel cartridge cases). Attempts were now geared towards making the shell more lethal, or improving the range of the gun by better shell design. Much work also went into studying methods of reducing the wear on the interior of the barrels that was caused by firing hundreds of shells through them, propelled by powders which had a flame temperature somewhat higher than the melting point of the barrel steel. 'Cooler' propellants offered a solution, but a cooler propellant generally produced less power than a hot one in the same quantity, requiring a larger powder charge. If the gun was already using a cartridge case stuffed to the brim with a hot propellant, the loss of performance caused by using the same amount of cool propellant was often unacceptable. Anti-tank and anti-aircraft guns rarely benefited from cooler propellants.

Work was also done on the search for a flashless propellant, since flash-spotting – the location of an enemy gun by cross-observation of the flash of discharge – was a well-tried method of countering enemy artillery. A flashless propellant would make counter-bombardment less likely. The question of flashless propellant became something of a compromise, however. The Royal Navy once defined 'flashless' as 'that degree of flash which will not attract the naked eye at 3,000 yards range' – sound enough in a naval context, but less acceptable in the case of field guns. Moreover, flashless propellants are, automatically, cooler propellants, leading to the problems associated with these, and they are also usually more sensitive to damp and generate more smoke. In addition, a propellant that was flashless in a 3in gun might often not be flashless in a 6in gun. One noted explosives expert said that the flashless, smokeless, noiseless explosive is usually powerless as well; it seems to be a valid point.

The First World War had shown artillerymen just how fast ammunition could be consumed by massed artillery firing for long periods of time. For example, between noon of 28 September 1918 and noon of 29 September 1918, the British artillery fired 943,847 shells. For the artilleryman, all those shells had somehow to be got to the guns; for the suppliers, all those shells had to be manufactured, and expensive methods of manufacture and exotic materials were not acceptable. Generally, shells were designed to be made from easily obtained material capable of being worked on easily obtained machinery. In Britain, this meant the adoption of '19-ton steel' as the standard shell material, an industrial grade of steel that could be handled by virtually any engineering shop. The drawback of this material was that the shell had to have rather thick walls in order to withstand the acceleration in the gun as it was fired, and thick walls meant a smaller cavity for the explosive and, hence, less explosive. The high-explosive filling in British field artillery shells averaged about 8 per cent of their overall weight. In the USA, 23-ton steel was the industrial norm; their shells had thinner walls, and the filling of TNT in the 105mm howitzer HE shell, for example, was 13 per cent of the total weight. This gave a more efficient burst, greater lethal radius and, all in all, 'a bigger bang for the money'.

The choice of steel was reflected in the choice of high explosive. The Americans tended to use Composition B, a mixture of RDX and TNT, whereas the British used straight TNT or Amatol, a mixture of TNT and ammonium nitrate. This was simply because 23-ton steel demanded a more violent explosive than 19-ton steel did in order to shatter it into suitably sized anti-personnel fragments. Using RDX/TNT with the lower-grade steel would have shattered it into relatively harmless powder instead of lethal fragments. Similarly, using Amatol in a 23-ton steel shell would have broken it into large fragments, individually highly lethal but incapable of covering the greater area achieved by the more powerful explosive.

TECHNIQUES

The actual technique of firing a gun so as to hit an unseen target remained unchanged from 1918; the angle between an identified point and the target was measured on a map, the sight line displaced by that angle, and the sight turned on to the aiming point so that the gun barrel pointed at the target. However, in order to be able to fire a collection of dispersed gun batteries at the same target, all the guns had to be precisely located on a common map grid system; picking the gun's position by six-figure grid reference off a one-inch map was not good enough, particularly if some guns were on different maps from others, and the maps were foreign and of doubtful accuracy.

Accurate surveying had to be done rapidly, as

American coast defence: a 14in gun in the Philippines being loaded

soon as the guns were in place; before it was done, they could do nothing but fire observed shots for their own observers. To achieve sufficient accuracy, military engineers provided surveyed points close behind the front line, forming part of a theatre-wide grid system. The gunners used these points to originate their own survey systems and produce coordinates for each 'pivot gun', the right-hand gun of each individual troop of four or six guns, or, in the case of heavy guns, for each gun. Once this was done, these points were plotted at a scale of 1:25,000 (2½in to one mile) on a blank gridded sheet of paper. Targets could now be plotted on the same grid system, based on grid references deduced by forward observers, and by firing data (azimuth and range). With every gun and every target on the same grid, ordering a grid reference to widely spaced guns now meant that there was a far greater chance that all their shells would fall in the same

spot, since they were all measuring from the same data. (These details refer to the British system; the American, French and Russian systems were similar.)

The raw data had then to be corrected to take into account wind, temperature, air density, and other physical changes that could affect the flight of the shell. These had been analysed and measured, and corrections had been established on experimental firing ranges in peacetime, and tabulated in books of data known as firing tables or range tables. The information about wind speed and air density was determined by sending up balloons every four hours and tracking them, deducing data and then circulating it to every artillery unit. This allowed 'predicted fire' to be employed; opening fire using data based upon the map and then corrected gave an even better chance of hitting the target with the first shot and, thus, of surprising an enemy. The

The war clouds gather. A British 3in AA gun on a Peerless lorry of First World War vintage, emplaced on Westminster Bridge during the Munich crisis of 1938

normal procedure – firing a ranging shot, correcting, firing another, correcting, and finally bringing in the remaining guns – alerted the enemy, so that, by the time the 'fire for effect' arrived, he was often in a deep shelter drinking coffee and playing cards. Predicted fire could catch him in the open and do substantial damage.

Shrapnel shell had become a thing of the past, except in some odd corners of the world and in some odd applications. Much to the relief of many gunners, the mind-boggling art of determining the correct fuze setting to burst the shell thirty feet above the enemy's head and some hundred yards or so in front of him, so as to drive the cone of shrapnel balls down at the right lethal angle, was relegated to history. In order to fulfil the need to strike down from the sky at men and equipment hiding behind cover, the time-fuzed high explosive 'airburst' shell came into use in place of shrapnel.

The fuze setting still had to be worked out, but it was far less critical than the fuze setting for shrapnel shell. (Incidentally, nobody has been wounded or killed by 'shrapnel' for more than fifty years, although the word is still much used by newspaper reporters.)

In September 1939, the gunners of various armies went to war and began to put into effect the techniques and tactics learned in peacetime. The next six years witnessed the fullest flowering of artillery power that the world has ever seen. And it is likely never to see it again. The massive concentrations of artillery used in 1939–45 could not last in the face of modern weapons, and the whole technique of artillery changed immensely after 1945. A study of the Allied artillery of the Second World War is, however, a study of artillery at its most powerful phase in history.

2 Field Artillery

'Field artillery' is a phrase that means different things to different armies. Generally, it describes the artillery which is part and parcel of the infantry or armoured division, acting as that division's immediate fire support, and subservient to the divisional commander. Other artillery may be attached, for special operations or to provide heavier support, and remains under the hand of a higher command.

'Field artillery' can also be used to describe the lighter forms of artillery that can be easily and quickly manoeuvred in support of tactical operations.

In another context, the phrase can be used to draw a line of limiting weight or calibre. This book deals more with the equipments than with the administration or organization, so for its purposes, and for organizational convenience, 'field artillery' encompasses all calibres up to and including 127mm/5in for guns and 150mm/6in for howitzers.

MECHANIZATION

Field artillery underwent a considerable change in the 1919–39 period, as a result of experience gained in 1914–1918. Prior to 1914, the ruling factor in field-gun design was the pulling power of a six-horse team. If the finest gun in the world was too heavy for six horses to move, it would not be adopted.

This attitude began to change in the late 1920s, as the motor vehicle took a grip on the civilian population, and the number of horses available for requisitioning to pull artillery in the event of war began rapidly to decrease. The armies were faced with either taking up horse-breeding as a full-time occupation, or embracing mechanical traction. A few might well have welcomed the former option, but fortunately common sense prevailed, and mechanization gradually began. (It is, however, a little-known fact that the only completely mechanized army that went to war in 1939 was the British. The French, German and Russian armies still relied very much on horse draught for their artillery and for much of their day-to-day transport in garrisons, and the US Army was still deploying horse cavalry as late as the summer of 1940.)

INCREASES IN CALIBRE

The second major factor for change, which links itself to the first, was the realization that the 75/76mm standard calibre of the First World War was no longer absolute. Most field pieces were of this calibre because of the weight; it was impossible to build a gun of a greater calibre without a heavier carriage and recoil system to withstand the stress, and thus with a dramatically increased weight. With less weight restriction, the designers could consider larger calibres, which meant more effective shells. As Lt Col A. Brooke RA (later Field Marshal Lord Alanbrooke) wrote in 1925, in a series of articles on the artillery lessons of the 1914–18 war, 'In peace the cry is for mobility, in war for weight of shell.' A heavier gun meant a heavier shell with a greater destructive power.

A heavier gun could also mean longer range, giving the gunners more leeway in selecting their gun positions; once in position, they could cover a greater area, and the number of guns needed to cover a given stretch of front could therefore be reduced. Reducing the number of guns meant reducing the number of gunners, leaving more men to spare for manning new and unfamiliar devices such as anti-tank and anti-aircraft guns. Mechanization was certainly to have some far-reaching effects.

TRENCH WARFARE AND THE HOWITZER

Another important factor was the change in the face of battle between 1914 and 1918. In 1914, soldiers marched in orderly columns towards the field of battle, sent out skirmishers, formed up in line, advanced in companies and, in general, manoeuvred in the open for much of the time. To counter this, field artillery was attuned to the rapid firing of shrapnel shells; these contained lead balls – about 300–350 to a 75mm shell was a good average figure – and were fuzed to burst in the air just above and in front of the target. The shell discharged its bullet, shotgun-fashion, down into the target area; if the target was a body of marching troops, the subsequent carnage was terrible.

By the middle of 1915, trench warfare had arrived, with dugouts, bomb-proof shelters, pillboxes and steel helmets, all intended to mitigate the effects of the shrapnel shell. (The steel helmets were, in fact, originally called 'shrapnel helmets'.) To deal with these protected troops, the high explosive shell was necessary, but to reach troops hiding in trenches or behind cover the high explosive shell had to be dropped quite steeply down. The pre-1914 gun, designed for shrapnel shooting, had a maximum elevation of about 15 degrees and simply could not drop shells steeply enough. That was the job of the howitzer, a short-barrelled gun which fired the shell into the air on a high trajectory so that it fell almost vertically.

Posed the post-war question 'Do you want a gun or a howitzer?' most armies would answer 'Both',

50th Field Battery RA show off their new Morris tractor and 18/25-pr gun in 1937, after their mechanization

but finances decreed otherwise in most cases. The solution was a compromise: the gun-howitzer. This weapon could fire at relatively high velocity and low trajectory in the gun role, but could also elevate high enough to act as a howitzer. It also had a cartridge system that was adjustable, to allow a selection of trajectories at lower velocities, so that the desired steep angle of descent at the target could be achieved at various ranges. Sometimes the weapon was called a gun (for example, the British 25-pounder), sometimes it was called a howitzer (like the American 105mm M1); sometimes it was described as a gun-howitzer (as with the Russian 152mm M10/37), but the name does not seem to have become part of any official terminology.

NEW DESIGNS FOR ARTILLERY

As a result of these various changes, armies began in the early 1920s to contemplate the replacement of their artillery. Designs were drawn, argued over, discarded, and re-drawn, and minor experiments were carried out, but behind all this was a universal shortage of money. The combatants of 1914–18 had wrecked their treasuries to pay for the war – believing that they were fighting the war to end all wars – and in the post-war years, social and commercial requirements had continued to make demands on funds. The easiest place to make economies in the aftermath of a major war is in the defence budget. Plans and drawings might be made, but the purse strings are kept very tight.

One favourable outcome of these financial restrictions was that the armies did not accept the first designs; they dissected and refined each one, and as a result the designs that appeared in the 1930s were generally excellent. They also gave themselves time to attend to the details that often get overlooked. Fuzes, fire-control instruments and communications were all examined closely, designs were perfected, prototypes were built and the designs stored away. Tactical theories were hammered out, tested on paper and on the ground, then modified and adopted.

In 1933, Adolf Hitler became Chancellor of Germany, repudiated the Versailles Treaty, and began re-arming. A new German Air Force began training, and warships and tanks began to be built. Gradually, as these activities became apparent, the democracies began to attend to their armament. Field artillery was low on the list of priorities. The pre-1939 bogies were air raids and poison gas, so air defence seemed more important. Eventually – and, as events proved, barely in time – field artillery began to appear from the factories. However, a great deal of equipment left over from 1918 remained in service; it had been paid for, and those who held the purse strings intended that it should be used as long as possible.

BRITAIN

Britain ended the First World War with a collection of field guns and howitzers, some of which dated from the Boer War. The first post-war task was to get rid of the weapons that were well past their useful life. This left only the 60-pounder gun, the 13-pr and 18-pr guns, and the 4.5in and 6in 26-cwt howitzers as service weapons. There was enough of them to allow some of the surplus to be sold to such emergent European countries as Latvia, Lithuania, Poland and Estonia, to outfit their newly formed armies.

The Search for a New Gun and Howitzer

Within three years of the war's end, the Royal Artillery was considering the replacement for the 18-pounder and the 4.5in howitzer. Ideally, it wanted a new gun and a new howitzer, but a realistic assessment of the stringent financial situation pointed to a single weapon capable of filling both roles. Also considered was a light field gun to arm new light batteries for the direct support of infantry.

The development of the 3in mortar, and its issue to the infantry, ended the idea of the light field gun. Since almost all available money and design

The 25-pr Gun Mark 1 (or 18/25pr) with ammunition trailer carrying the traversing platform. This picture is rather odd, because a split-trail carriage did not really need a platform

facilities were being pointed in the direction of Singapore, not much came out of the field gun/howitzer discussion either.

In 1925, the designers were told that for future designs they might contemplate mechanical traction, and exceed the long-standing weight limit linked to the use of a six-horse team. On the other side of the coin, they were also asked to produce a gun with a range of 15,000 yards (13,760m), with a split-trail carriage, to give the gun a wide arc of fire for anti-tank defence. There were even suggestions that 80 degrees of elevation would be useful, so that the gun could double as an anti-aircraft gun.

Vickers produced a rather pedestrian design for a 105mm howitzer firing bag charges and with a box trail; this was a sound enough weapon but it was not a 15,000-yard gun with wide traverse and all the bells and whistles, so it was refused. The Royal Gun Factory came up with a design for a 100mm gun, which promised only 11,900 yards (10,920m), so that was not accepted either. Then there was a change of policy.

The Gun-Howitzer

It had been increasingly obvious that a new gun to replace the 18-pr and a new howitzer to replace the

4.5in was too much for the Treasury to swallow; one of them would have to go. The idea of the 'gun-howitzer' began to be seen some time in 1928. After reviewing the various designs that had been offered and prototype guns that had been tested, the Director of Artillery Maj-Gen H.A. Lewis put forward a proposal for a new 3.7in (94mm) gun-howitzer to fire a 25lb (11.35kg) shell. After this came discussions with the General Staff, in which this '25-pounder' gun was proposed as the future sole armament of field regiments (of which some had guns and some had howitzers). An agreement having been reached, in September 1934 the Director of Artillery ordered construction of the first prototype.

Finance was still scarce, so the design had to be modified to use as much existing equipment as possible. One economizing idea was to put the new gun barrel on top of the existing modernized 18-pr carriages, but in 3.7in calibre it was impossible. The calibre was therefore reduced to 3.45in, and this allowed the manufacture of a barrel which would fit into the jacket of the old 18-pr, accept the 18-pr breech fittings and mechanism, and could thus be fitted on to the old carriages. However, at the same time as accepting this compromise,

General Lewis also made sure that the designers were working on a totally new carriage for future production when money became available.

The new equipment was formally introduced into service as the 'Ordnance, QF, 3.45in Mark I' on 26 August 1936, the guns being fitted to either the box-trail Mark 3 or split-trail Mark 5 18-pr carriages. In February 1938, the nomenclature was officially changed to 'Ordnance QF, 25-pr Mark I', but no one ever referred to them in that way. To the gunners, they were always the 'eighteen/twenty-five pounders'. Just over one thousand of them were built.

Carriage Design

The designers of the new carriage produced a surprising collection of advanced ideas, including a three-legged platform allowing all-round traverse, a four-wheeled carriage in which the wheels turned inwards to allow it to traverse quickly and easily, and a split-trail carriage. Numerous ideas were mocked up and tried, but eventually the Royal Gun Factory and Vickers both produced split-trail solutions. Prototypes were made and supplied for trial, but the response to both from the gunners was not favourable.

One of the drawbacks of a split-trail design is the length of the trail legs. The working length of a box- or pole-trail – the distance from the axle to the spade – is calculated to resist the turning moment around the spade cause by the force of the recoiling gun. If this is, say, seven feet, there is a seven-foot trail. With a split trail, if the measurement from the axle to the spade with the trail open is seven feet, when the trail is swung and the two legs are closed for travelling, the trail will be about nine feet long. Those extra two feet of steel add weight and length, and upset the balance about the axle, making the gun hard to manhandle.

The gunners objected to the split-trail design because of its clumsiness, weight and general inconvenience in operation. An appeal was made to the Superintendent of Design, Major-General Macrae, for a fresh design to be drawn up, but

Macrae realized that this would take up valuable time when war clouds were gathering. In order to provide an alternative design, he proposed to mount the 25-pr gun on top of the box-trail carriage that Vickers had designed for their abandoned 105mm howitzer. Beneath it there would be a circular platform, devised in 1918 for the 18-pr gun, which would allow the whole gun to be swung rapidly around in the hunt for tanks.

This concept was rapidly put together and early in 1938 a comparative test of three carriage designs was carried out at the School of Artillery at Larkhill in Wiltshire. After the weapons had been demonstrated to an audience of senior gunner officers, a conference was held and, on a show of hands, the box-trail design was chosen over the split-trail.

The Mark 2 25-Pounder

The completely new design of gun – the same gun barrel but with a new breech mechanism – was officially introduced as the Mark 2 25-pounder in December 1937. The new carriage had to be properly re-designed after the hurried make-over that had been used as a demonstrator, and it was not approved until late in 1939. At the outbreak of war there were only seventy-eight guns and no carriages. The British Expeditionary Force went to France with the 18/25-pounder, and a Canadian regiment, the 8th Army Field Regiment RCA, received the first Mark 2 25-pounder issued in April 1940.

The only major modification ever made to the 25-pr gun was the addition of a muzzle brake in 1942; until then, the AP shot had been fired with the super charge alone. With the adoption of a muzzle brake, a 'super increment' could be fired, since the brake reduced the stress on the recoil system. This gave that extra bit of armour-defeating performance that was vital against German tanks. (The Australians and New Zealanders did not fit the muzzle brake, since they could deal quite effectively with Japanese tanks without the extra boost.)

A 105mm howitzer developed by Vickers in 1930; when the split-trail 25-pr design was disliked by the users, it was the trail and platform from this design which became the 25-pr carriage

One of the suggested designs for the 25-pr gun

The wooden mock-up of the split-trail carriage 25-pr gun

New Carriage Designs

With the introduction of air transportation, it was soon discovered that, while the Dakota aircraft could lift the 25-pounder, its wheel track was too big to allow the gun to be loaded through the side door and turned into the fuselage. It was necessary to remove the shield and axle and lift the cradle and gun so that everything could be lifted and shoved aboard by manpower. The Canadians developed a Mark 3 carriage, with a shorter axle (the same track width as a jeep, and therefore a convenient size for jeep towing in jungle trails), and a hinge in the middle of the trail, which allowed the trail to be dropped to give the gun another 30 degrees of elevation. A smaller shield and smaller platform, and a special sight bracket, completed the design, and it was possible to load this straight into the door of the Dakota, turn it into the fuselage and lash it down.

The Australians, faced with the worst terrain in the world – the New Guinea mountains and jungle – developed the '25-pr Short Mark I (Australian)'. The object was to produce a pack-transportable weapon, and this entailed radical surgery. The trail was a greatly simplified girder structure, the wheels were smaller, there was no shield and no platform but a massive spade, and the trail had a castor wheel to help in manhandling. The gun was drastically cut down to just under 50in in length; when it was fired, the muzzle flash burned the rods of the recoil system as the cradle moved back, so a conical flash shroud had to be attached to the muzzle. The gun was much lighter than standard, and it could not be fired with super charge, as it would recoil too fast and build up excessive pressure in the recoil system. Charge Three was the maximum, giving a range of 10,800 yards (9,910m). The equipment could be broken down into 14 mule loads.

Ordnance, QF, 25-pr Gun Marks 1, 2 and 3

In post-war analyses of lessons learned through the First World War, the Royal Artillery decided that both their standard field gun, the 18-pr, and the field howitzer, the 4.5-in, should be replaced with new weapons. A number of possible designs were studied during the 1920s, but eventually financial stringency suggested that a single weapon would have to replace both, and the idea of a gun-howitzer was approached. This appeared in prototype form in 1934, but the process was further complicated by the demand that the design should use as many existing parts of the 18-pr as possible. The final design was a 3.45in gun barrel slipped into the existing jacket of the 18-pr gun. It was introduced as the 25-pr Gun Mark 1 in February 1938.

The Mark 2, a completely new design of gun and carriage, took time to perfect and get into production, becoming general issue towards the end of 1940.

The 25-pounder was a classic design; it was enormously robust, and, if anything ever did go wrong, it could be repaired in the field with the simplest of tools. It was light enough to be manhandled by six men, yet powerful enough to range to 13,400 yards. The ammunition was separate-loading – the shell was loaded and rammed, the brass-cased cartridge loaded behind it, and the vertical sliding-block breech manually closed. The cartridge case held three bags of propellant and could be fired with one, two or three bags, to give Charge One, Two or Three; this 'zoning' of the charge gave the weapon its howitzer characteristics, allowing it to fire on a high trajectory to clear hills or other obstacles and drop shells steeply into places a pure gun could never reach. In Italy and other mountainous countries, 'incremental charges' were introduced. These were small bags of propellant, which could be used with charges one and two to give Charge 1½, Charge 2⅓ and Charge 2⅔. Above Charge Three came Charge Super, but this was non-adjustable and provided the 'gun' element of the performance, a fixed long-range charge. Finally, an incremental charge could be added to Charge Super, to gain a little extra velocity when firing the armour-piercing shot, which, since it weighed 20lb instead of the normal 25lb, could be given a more powerful charge without exceeding the safe pressure limits. The muzzle brake was added to reduce the recoil impulse when firing AP Shot at Super-plus charge, and it naturally had a good effect with every other charge, making the gun very stable.

The Mark 3 carriage was hinged in the middle of the trail, so that an extra 30 degrees of elevation could be achieved, to give even greater flexibility in the howitzer role and permit 'upper register' firing (the term at the time for firing at angles greater than 45 degrees). (For the 'Short 25-pr', *see* page 26.) It was also proposed, at various times, as a submarine gun, a shore bombardment gun for light naval craft, fitted to a Bren gun carrier as a self-propelled weapon, and as the primary armament for the Australian 'Sentinel' tank. It was a most versatile weapon, and is still in use, in India and Pakistan, in 1998.

DATA: (Mark 2 Gun on Mark 2 Carriage)

Calibre	3.45in (87mm)
Weight of gun and breech	10cwt 0qr 4lb (510kg) with muzzle brake and counterweight
Total weight in action	3,968lb (1,800kg)
Barrel length	97.47in (2.47m); 106.72in (2.71m) with muzzle brake
Rifling	26 grooves, right-hand twist, one turn in 20 calibres
Recoil system and length	Hydro-pneumatic, variable, 20 to 44in (508 to 1,117mm)
Breech mechanism	Vertical sliding block, manual; percussion firing
Elevation	-5 to +40 degrees
Traverse	4 degrees either side of zero
Shell weight	25lb (11.34kg)
Muzzle velocity	1,700ft/sec (518m/sec)
Maximum range	13,400 yards (12,252m) Charge Super
Types of projectile available	HE; HE with tracer; AP shot; BE smoke, coloured smoke, coloured flare, illuminating star, incendiary, radar echo, chemical, propaganda leaflet

Ordnance, QF, 25-pr Gun Marks 1, 2 and 3 continued

Painted and polished to perfection, a 25-pr gun on Mark 2 carriage; note the firing platform and the 'banana box' under the spade to prevent it digging in when fired on the platform. This is a post-war picture; the reflectors on the shield were not seen before the 1950s

But for the headgear, this could be a wartime picture; anti-tank practice on Salisbury Plain, 1953

Guns in war are not quite such a picture of perfection as guns in peacetime; here, a 25-pr detachment wends its way through Italy in 1943. Note the dragropes on the shield, camouflage nets on the trailer, and the worldly goods on the back of the tractor

The 25-pr Mark 3 carriage in use; the hinged trail can be seen, together with the pit necessary to permit the full recoil stroke, since the automatic adjustment was 'fooled' by the additional elevation

The 'Short' or 'Baby' 25-pr gun, without the caster wheel on the trail

Front view of the Short 25-pr gun, showing the use of 'firing segments' below the axle to take the firing shock off the tyres

The 25-pr MARC – Mobile Armoured Revolving Carriage – was a Canadian idea, which amounted to a mobile pillbox. It was not pursued

Having studied this weapon, the British produced a similar design, but with modifications to the recoil system to permit firing Charge Super. It was officially approved as the Mark 4 in May 1945, by which time it had become obvious that there was no real need for it; only one or two were made and it was declared obsolete in 1946.

The 4.5in Howitzer

The 25-pounder had replaced the 18-pounder in the field-gun role. The intention was that it should also replace the 4.5in howitzer in the field howitzer slot, but in the early days production was slow, and several batteries of 4.5in howitzers went to France in 1939 and fought the 1940 campaign. Others were used in the Eritrean campaign and in the Western Desert in 1940-42. It was not until the end of the North African campaign in 1943 that the 4.5in howitzer was withdrawn from field formations, after which it was retained solely as a training weapon until all its ammunition had been used up. That happened in the run-up to D-Day, and the howitzer and all its stores were declared obsolete in September 1944.

The 4.5in howitzer had been introduced in 1909, after a series of trials of designs from various gunmakers. The selected design had been produced by the Coventry Ordnance Works, a consortium of shipbuilding and engineering companies led by William Beardmore & Co in a bid to break the duopoly of commercial gun-making enjoyed by Vickers and Armstrong. Their original intention was to break into the naval gun market, but they were just in time to reap the benefit of the post-Boer War armament programmes. After cutting their teeth on production of components for the 18-pr gun, they had a major success with the 4.5in howitzer and went on to do more useful work before collapsing in the between-wars slump.

In its original form, with wooden wheels, the 4.5in looked rather old-fashioned, but between the wars its appearance was considerably improved by the fitting of steel wheels with pneumatic tyres. This was, in fact, the only major modification ever made to it; the original design had been right, in that it did what it was asked and did it reliably. There was no room for improvement without major re-design, so the howitzer itself saw no changes. It fired a 35lb (15.6kg) shell to a maximum range of only 7,000 yards (6,675m) and was also provided with shrapnel, parachute star and two types of smoke shell, but the lack of range told against it and was the principal reason for its retirement.

The 6in Howitzer

The heaviest British howitzer in this class was the 6in 26-cwt weapon; the addition of the barrel's

Sea-going artillery; a 25-pr mounted on a DUKW amphibious truck as an offshore bombardment support weapon – another idea that failed to gain many followers

Rear view of the 4.5in howitzer; apart from the wheels and pneumatic tyres, it was the same in 1939 as it had been in 1909

Front view of the 4.5in howitzer, revealing how the suspension had to be modified to accommodate the smaller wheels

weight to the name was a reminder that there had been two other howitzers of this calibre but of different weights at the time of its introduction. Even though these were long obsolete, the identification remained part of the name. The 6in 26-cwt had appeared in 1915 and rapidly became one of the most useful guns in the army, with over 3,000 being made before 1919. It was modernized in the 1930s, by the fitting of a new axle with steel wheels and pneumatic tyres, and it fired a 100lb (45kg) shell to 9,500 yards (8,710m) or a lighter 86lb (39kg) shell to 11,400 yards (10,460m). This had been considered a good performance in 1918 but by 1939 it was falling behind in the race; although those in service saw some use in the African campaigns, they were gradually replaced by the 5.5in gun.

The 6in howitzer was retained as a training weapon, and finally declared obsolete in October 1945.

The 60-Pounder

The other First World War veteran to be classed as a field weapon was the 60-pounder (5in/127mm calibre) gun which had first appeared in 1904. A cumbersome weapon by modern standards, it was considered obsolescent by 1939 and was scheduled to be replaced by the 4.5in and 5.5in guns. As with everything else, production was slow and the 60-pr stayed in service. Many were converted to 4.5in guns Mark I (*see* page 35), but a number were left unconverted and used in the North African campaigns. In common with the 4.5in howitzer, the end of the campaign in North Africa saw the 60-pounder's retirement from active service and its relegation to a training role until its stock of ammunition was used up. It was declared obsolete on 8 June 1944.

The 60-pr went through a series of modifications during its early wartime life and by 1918 the standard was the Mark 2 gun on Mark 4 carriage. It

The 6in 26-cwt howitzer was another First World War weapon that had been 'pneumatized' in the 1930s

Highland games: a Scottish Territorial regiment at drill with their 6in howitzers in 1942. This ritual was the easiest and quickest way to get the rammer back to the gun Number One so that Numbers Five and Six (standing in the trail) could get it out of the way, and remove the loading tray from the cradle

was a two-wheeled carriage with a large box-trail, similar in some respects to that of the 25-pr gun but considerably larger. The gun sat on a top carriage, slung in a cradle. For travelling, the trail end was supported on a two-wheeled limber, and the gun and recoil system were pulled back in the cradle, to distribute the weight between the four wheels and reduce the length of the equipment. For mechanical traction it had large steel and wood wheels with solid tyres. It fired a 60lb (22.25kg) shell to a range of 16,400 yards (15,045m) and used a non-adjustable bag charge.

In 1922, it was proposed to improve the 60-pr gun by removing the barrel and putting a 4.5in barrel in its place. This, with a modern streamlined shell was expected to improve the range. Given the financial strain, it is no surprise that the proposed re-design eventually meant re-lining the barrel to 4.5in calibre. A prototype was tested in 1937 and gave a range of 20,000 yards (18,350m), and the

conversion was approved. It was then discovered that there were no more than seventy-six 60-pr guns available for conversion, which was scarcely sufficient to equip the peacetime army, let alone an expanded wartime force.

In 1938, the Director of Artillery, on his own responsibility, ordered the design of a completely new 4.5in gun, dimensioned to fit the carriage then being prepared for a new 5.5in weapon. The design was prepared and approved on 31 August 1939, but no production was possible until late in 1940 and the first guns were issued early in 1941.

Except for its barrel, the 4.5in gun Mark 2 was identical to the 5.5in Mark 3, with the same carriage and breech mechanism being used on both. The 4.5in fired a 55lb (25kg) shell to a range of 20,500 yards (18,800m), using a three-increment bag charge. It was a reliable gun, but generally thought to be too much gun for too little shell, and the extra range was not really sufficient

Deadly earnest: a 6in howitzer in action on the Western Desert in 1941. Note the Number One holding the rammer, and the next shell on the loading tray on the rear end of the trail

One of the last 60-pr guns in action at Tobruk, 1941, manned by Australian gunners

The 4.5in BL gun shared the same carriage with the 5.5in; only the barrel length is different

compensation for the lightweight shell. The Mark I guns (the converted 60-pr weapon) were obsolete in April 1944; the Mark 2 gun lingered until late 1959, but it was entirely a training weapon in post-war years.

The 3.7in Howitzer

The last of the British field equipments was the 3.7in howitzer, variously called 'mountain' or 'pack', although neither word featured in the official nomenclature. This gun had been developed by Vickers in 1910, at the request of the Indian government. Shortage of money led to it being shelved until 1916, when it went into production to replace a variety of elderly 'screw-guns' being used by Indian Army mountain artillery batteries.

The 'screw-gun' of which Kipling wrote was properly known as the 'Ordnance, Jointed, Rifled Muzzle Loading, 2.5in' and was invented in 1879 by a Col Le Mesurier, RA. He took the idea to Sir William Armstrong and the gun was developed.

The aim was simply to obtain a useful length of barrel, within the constraints imposed by mule carriage; a mule would carry up to about 200lb (91kg) in weight before balking, so the weapon had to dismantle into 200lb pieces. A barrel of reasonable length was more than 200lb, so by breaking the gun in two, you could arrive at a 400lb (181.8kg) gun without breaking the mule's back. The barrel was divided about halfway along its length; the rear end carried the breech mechanism and the front end carried the 'junction nut', which screwed the two parts together. The idea proved to be a success and the principle was refined and improved through a series of weapons, of which the last was the 3.7in of 1916.

The 3.7in carriage was the first split-trail pattern to be adopted by the British, and it gave the howitzer a wide traversing arc without the need to shift the trail bodily. As most of its work was on the north-west frontier of India, it had a sizeable shield to protect the gunners; it had a modern hydro-pneumatic recoil system, and in the between-wars

Loading a 4.5in gun, Normandy, 1944. Note No 6 waiting with the bag charge, Nos 1, 4 and 5 ramming, No 2 loading the firing lock, and No 3 standing clear until the gun is loaded before returning to his sights for a quick check. The contorted figure on the right is an Army Film Unit cameraman recording the action. This wartime picture has had the badges and formation signs on the uniforms painted out

period it was given pneumatic-tyred wheels. The howitzer fired a 20lb (9kg) HE shell to a maximum range of 4,500 yards (4,130m); when shrapnel was in vogue it fired a 20lb (9kg) shrapnel shell to 6,000 yards (5,500m).

In the 1939-45 period it was mostly used in the Far East, with numerous mountain batteries being deployed in Burma; it also appeared in the more rugged parts of East Africa and North Africa, and

Italy. It was also adopted by airborne formations (although these later adopted the American 75mm howitzer, which was lighter). Perhaps its least-known employment was with the Royal Marines, as a landing gun for shore duties.

The 3.7 remained in service after the war, but its days were numbered. In mid-1944, a specification was issued for a 3.3in howitzer firing an 18lb (8.2kg) shell to replace it, and the

A 3.7in mountain howitzer complete with its rarely seen ammunition trailer, only used with motor transport

The 3.7in howitzer in action; note the substantial shield and the spades, which could be driven in with sledge-hammers

Indian mountain gunners of the 14th Army with their 3.7in howitzer in Burma, 1944

development of this occupied the Canadian Army on and off until the middle 1950s, before it was finally decided that there was no modern requirement for it. The 3.7in was finally declared obsolete in February 1960.

THE USA

The Westervelt Board

> Para. 142. A Board of Officers to consist of Brig Gens William I. Westervelt, Robert E. Callan, William P. Ennis, Cols James B. Dillard, Ralph McT. Penell, and Lt Cols Webster A. Capron and Walter P. Boatwright, US Army, is appointed to meet at APO 706, France, at the earliest practicable date, to make a study of the armament, calibers and types of materiel, kinds and proportions of ammunition and methods of transport of the artillery to be assigned to a Field Army... By order of the Secretary of War. Peyton C. March, General, Chief of Staff.

(Extract from US Army Special Order 289–0, 11 December 1918.)

This special order was the genesis of the 'Caliber Board', as it was called at the time, or the 'Westervelt Board', as it eventually came to be known. It was a well-selected board. Of these officers, Westervelt became Chief of Staff,

Boatwright Chief of Artillery, and the others distinguished themselves equally in their various fields. They assembled at Chaumont on 12 January 1919, visited French, Italian and British headquarters and ordnance factories, returned to the USA to visit factories and artillery establishments, and submitted their report on 5 May 1919. The report runs to thirty-eight pages and there is scarcely one superfluous word. First, the report considered what the artillery of a field army was supposed to do, then it laid out an organization capable of doing it, and then it detailed exactly what sort of weapons were needed to do it.

The Westervelt Board was convened so that the development of the field artillery arm over the next twenty years could be planned. The US Army's field artillery had been a minority arm until 1917. It then had to undergo massive expansion, and in doing so found that its equipment was not capable, in terms of both quantity and quality, of providing the support the army needed. As a result, all but a handful of its guns were provided by Britain and France, and its artillery doctrines were almost entirely dictated by the French Army.

Once the war was over, the US field artillery set about taking control of its own affairs; prior to 1917, it had such minor status that the Ordnance Department told it what guns it was going to have, and Infantry told it what to do with them. The wartime expansion gave it a Chief of Artillery,

General Snow, with sufficient clout to argue for it in Washington.

Regarding equipment, the board reached the conclusion that what was needed was a light gun of about 3in/75mm calibre, firing a 15lb (6.8kg) shell to 11,000 yards (10,090m), backed up by a howitzer of about 4in/105mm calibre firing a 25- to 30lb (11.35-13.65kg) shell to a range in excess of 10,000 yards (9,200m). A 'medium field gun' with a calibre somewhere between three and six inches was also considered necessary, the board pointing to the British 60-pounder and similar French and German weapons. For a medium field howitzer, the French 155mm Schneider was considered perfectly satisfactory, and it continued in service as the M1917. A heavy field gun of about 6in and a heavy howitzer of about 9.5in were next on the list of requirements, which ended with four major-calibre support weapons: an 8in gun firing to 35,000 yards (32,110m); a 14in gun firing to 40,000 yards (36,700m); a 12in howitzer firing to 25,000 yards (22,940m); and a 16in howitzer with a range not less than 27,000 yards (22,770m). This latter group were all to be mounted on railway carriages.

The light field equipments were then considered in more detail. The 'ideal solution' for the howitzer was described as follows: 'A weapon of about 105mm caliber on a carriage permitting a vertical arc of fire from minus 5 degrees to plus 65 degrees, and a horizontal arc of fire of 360 degrees. The projectile should weigh about 30 to 35 pounds and should include shrapnel and shell. A maximum range of 12,000 yards will be satisfactory. Semi-fixed ammunition and zone charges should be used.'

For the light field gun they requested 'a gun of about 3in caliber on a carriage permitting a vertical arc of fire of from minus 5 degrees to plus 80 degrees and a horizontal arc of fire of 360 degrees; a projectile weighing not over 20 pounds, shrapnel and high explosive shell; fixed ammunition; smokeless, flashless propelling charge; time fuze for shrapnel; bore-safe, super-quick and selective delay fuze for shell. . . Two propelling charges should be furnished, a normal charge for about

11,000 yards range and a super-charge for maximum range. A maximum rate of fire of 20 rounds per minute is deemed sufficient.'

These were the ideal solutions. The 'practical' solutions were simple – continue to use the war's leftovers until the research departments came up with the ideals – and that was exactly what happened.

Both the light field gun and the howitzer were to have 'a horizontal arc of fire of 360 degrees', and the gun was to have a maximum elevation of 80 degrees, whereas the howitzer would only reach 65 degrees. As far as the howitzer was concerned, the 360-degree part was fairly rapidly abandoned, since it must have become obvious that a carriage capable of all-round fire would be excessively heavy in that calibre.

The two figures quoted for the gun gave rise to a long and fruitless pursuit of the all-purpose gun, the '75mm Light Divisional Gun'. This had a three-legged trail carrying a pedestal-mounted 75mm gun with a very long barrel; the general effect was an anti-aircraft gun capable of operating in the ground role rather than a field gun capable of anti-aircraft fire. It is not clear exactly when and why this idea was finally knocked on the head; it was certainly being illustrated in military magazines in 1935, but in 1938, Hayes' *Elements of Ordnance*, the official West Point text on artillery, said 'the so-called all-purpose mounts, designed for several classes of fire requiring several types of materiel, have not proved successful or practicable.' This seems to suggest that the light divisional gun had been abandoned.

However, while this wild goose chase was in progress, a great deal of more substantial work had been done.

The 75mm Howitzer

The 75mm Gun M1897, the original French 75 adopted in 1917, had remained the standard field gun ever since, and it had been slightly modified over the years. By 1939, it had reached the M1897A4 model of gun and the M2A3 carriage. The gun had the muzzle rollers removed and the

The 75mm Light Divisional Gun in 1935. With a third trail leg added under the barrel, and the wheels removed, this became a field gun with 360 degrees of traverse and 85 degrees of elevation, which could double as an anti-aircraft gun. It was a good theory, but not so good in practice, so it was dropped

breech-block altered to give a 156-degree opening and closing movement instead of the original 120 degrees, and the carriage had been changed into a split-trail with steel wheels, pneumatic tyres, a small shield and some minor modifications to suit the improved gun. The weight of the equipment had gone up from 2,657lb (1,207.75kg) to 3,225lb (1,466kg), but the maximum range had gone from 9,200 yards (8,440m) to 13,950 yards (12,800m) with a 14.7lb (6.7kg) shell. This was fairly close to the Westervelt's ideal gun, and the army seems to have been quite happy with it.

The 75mm howitzer had been designed during the 1920s to meet a requirement put forward by the Westervelt Board for a mountain and pack gun as an urgent necessity. The urgency was met by producing the first pattern in 1920, but this proved too hasty and a fresh design appeared in 1922. After some minor changes, this was standardized as the 'Howitzer, Pack, 75mm M1 on Carriage M1', in 1927. It was an ingenious design which stripped into four mule-loads and could fire the same shell as the 75mm field gun, to a range of 9,600 yards (8,810m), well in excess of the range required by the board. In its original form, it had the usual wooden wheels of the period, but when the US Army began contemplating airborne troops, a new

carriage with steel wheels and pneumatic tyres was produced as the M8.

The performance of the 75mm howitzer was so good that in the late 1920s it was decided to produce a non-dismantling carriage and issue it as a cavalry support gun. This became the Howitzer M1 on Carriage M3. The carriage had a split-trail, a firing jack to support the axle, twin balancing springs and a shield – a very luxurious product. However, very few appear to have been made; by the time the design was standardized, horse cavalry was looking into tanks, and their accompanying artillery into self-propelled guns.

The 'Ideal' Field Howitzer

Development of the Westervelt Board's ideal field howitzer began in 1920 with the production of four pilot models of the Howitzer, 105mm M1920 on Carriage M1920E. They all had slight differences, but common to all of them was a 22-calibre long gun with horizontal sliding breech-block, a split trail, 80-degree elevation and 30-degree traverse. There was also a Carriage M1921E, which was a box-trail, giving 51-degree elevation and 8-degree traverse. The Field Artillery Board looked at all these, tested them, and threw out all the M1920E

75mm Gun M1897

This French gun was adopted by the US Army in 1917 as an expedient, pending the development of its own M1916 design. In the event, the M1916 was a failure, and the M1897 became its standard field piece. It should have been scrapped after 1918, but by that time the wartime manufacturing contracts were only just beginning to produce guns, so the army had little choice but to perpetuate it in service. The development of the 105mm howitzer proves that they realized the correct solution, but no army could afford to throw away guns in the lean years between 1918 and 1939. The M1897 was constantly being worked on, with small improvements being added as and when they could be afforded, until the basic design had been exploited as far as possible; the result was a weapon far superior to the French one first seen in 1917.

The M1897 gun was the original French design, with a muzzle velocity of 529m/sec (1,735ft/sec) and a maximum range of 8,500m (9,295 yds). The M1897A1 was the same, but made in the USA. The M1897A2 did away with the jacket and had an autofrettaged one-piece barrel; the breech mechanism was altered so that the handle and screw rotated through 156 degrees instead of 120 degrees, which gave better leverage for extracting sticky cartridge cases. The M1897A3 was the same as the A2, but with some slight modifications to suit it to the M1897M1A2 carriage. Finally, on the M1897A4, the muzzle-rollers (which engaged in the cradle and supported the muzzle weight during recoil) were removed, and replaced by steel rails and bronze strips.

The M1897 carriage was the original French two-wheeled pole-trail design, and the M1897M1 was the American-made version, with some small changes for production convenience. The M1897A2 was an M1897 fitted with a traversing handspike (why the French never used one is a mystery), and the M1897M1A2 was the American carriage with handspike added. The M1897A3 was not adopted, and the design has been forgotten. The M1897A4 was any previous carriage fitted with the 'high-speed adapter', in other words, rubber-tyred wheels and drum brakes.

Then came a completely fresh design of split-trail carriage, the M2. This had pneumatic tyres, a firing jack under the axle, no shield, and a new recoil system giving variable length recoil according to the gun's elevation. The M2A1 had the shield put back and some changes to the brakes, and the M2A2 made more changes to the axle and brakes. Finally, the M2A3 went back to a constant-length recoil system, fitted a pivoted axle, shortened the trail by 19in, and removed the firing jack, replacing it by 'firing segments', which were wedge-shaped steel pieces that revolved on the axles and, when dropped down, took the weight off the tyres, and made the gun more stable.

The final combination was the M1897A4 gun on the M2A3 carriage; the various weapon improvements, allied to improvements in shell design and propellant charges, had improved the muzzle velocity to 596m/sec (1,955ft/sec), and the maximum range to 12,756 metres (13,950 yards).

DATA (M1897A4 Gun on Carriage M2A3)

Calibre	75mm (2.95in)
Weight of gun and breech	1,035lb (470kg)
Total weight in action	3,675lb (1,667kg)
Barrel length	107.13in (2.72m)
Rifling	24 grooves, right-hand, one turn in 25.6 calibres
Recoil system and length	Hydro-pneumatic, constant, 44.9in (1,140mm)
Breech mechanism	Nordenfelt eccentric screw, percussion firing
Elevation	-9 degrees 15' to + 49 degrees 30'
Traverse	30 degrees left and right of zero
Shell weight	14.6lb (6.62kg)
Muzzle velocity	1,955ft/sec (596m/sec)
Maximum range	13,950 yards (12,756m)
Types of projectile available	HE; WP Smoke; AP/HE Capped

75mm Gun M1897 continued

My, how you've grown! Twenty years of improvement produced the M1897A4, on Carriage M2A3, the ultimate 'French 75' for the US Field Artillery

The 75mm howitzer M2, intended for use with the cavalry, had a split trail and a firing pedestal, seen here folded up beneath the barrel

carriages as being too complicated and heavy.

More work produced the Howitzer M1925E on Carriage M1925E, a second box-trail design, in response to the Field Artillery Board's ideas. Rock Island Arsenal had ideas of their own, and produced the Howitzer T2 on Carriage T2, another split-trail

The 75mm howitzer M1 was the pack artillery version, with lightweight box trail and wooden wheels

The 75mm howitzer M8 was the rubber-tyred version, used by airborne artillery in both US and British formations

design. This so impressed the FA Board that the M1925E was dumped, and the T2 was standardized as the Howitzer M1 on Carriage M1 in January 1928. It used a seven-zone charge and fired a 33lb (15kg) shell to 12,000 yards (11,000m).

Very few M1 equipments were built; no sooner was the design standardized than it was frozen, simply because there was no money available to build it. The design was prepared for production, and put away in the safe.

At about this time, the US Army began thinking about mechanization, which meant, among other things, re-designing gun carriages for high-speed towing. The 105mm howitzer carriage was

The 105mm howitzer M1, with wooden wheels for horse draught. The spring balancing apparatus beneath the cradle can be seen quite clearly

Figure 1.
105 mm ...

The 105mm howitzer M1 at maximum elevation

scheduled for re-design in 1933, but it did not get on to the drawing board until 1936. When the designers began to contemplate modifying the M1 carriage, they soon realized it would be easier to tear up the drawings and start afresh. This led to the T3, T4 and T5 carriages, the last of which was standardized as the M2 carriage in February 1940.

Meanwhile, the gun had been modified as well. It had been designed with semi-fixed ammunition, where the shell could be removed from the cartridge case in order to adjust the charge, but replaced so as to be loaded into the gun as one unit. In 1933, it was decided to make the shrapnel round fixed and non-adjustable; this meant that some minor changes to the internal contour of the gun chamber had to be made, and the result was standardized as the 'Howitzer 105mm M2' in April 1934. A year later, the approval was rescinded, as the shrapnel shell was no longer classed as the primary projectile, its place being taken by the high explosive shell.

Nevertheless, the M2 remained the standard, and, in the course of adapting the gun to fit the T5/M1 carriage, some more small changes were made, so that the final design was standardized as the Howitzer M2A1 in March 1940. Production began immediately and 8,536 were built during the war years. There were some very small modifications from time to time, and, in revised form, it has remained the standard field artillery piece of the US Army ever since.

105mm Howitzer M2A1

Although it is generally, and rightly, said that the American 105mm howitzer owes its existence to the Westervelt Board, the idea of a 105mm weapon goes back further. In 1916, Colonel Charles P. Summerall of the US Army was sent to France by the Secretary of War, Newton Baker. He was required to observe and report on the development of military equipment by the European armies, in order to guide future American weapon design and procurement policy. One of Summerall's recommendations was that the 75mm/3in class of field gun was now out-dated, and no longer powerful enough, and that the future US field artillery weapon should be of 105mm calibre. At that time, the Ordnance Department still made final decisions over artillery equipment, and Summerall was ignored. However, it is a fair assumption that the Westervelt Board got hold of Summerall's report during their deliberations, and saw that his idea made sense.

The development of the 105mm Howitzer M1 is detailed elsewhere. The howitzer itself was a simple and straightforward design, using semi-fixed ammunition; the cartridge contained a seven-part charge in seven cloth bags. The base charge was secured to the bottom of the cartridge case, and the other bags were attached by twine, so that the unwanted bags could be snapped off and discarded. HE and WP Smoke were the two original projectiles, shrapnel having been abandoned in 1935, but in 1941 a base ejection smoke shell appeared, copied from the British 25-pounder shell. Then came a shaped-charge anti-tank shell, coloured smoke, and a canister shot round, which was found particularly useful in the South Pacific for shredding the undergrowth and tree-tops to flush out Japanese snipers.

The carriage was a two-wheeled split-trail pattern, and the gun was trunnioned as far back as possible so that the breech would not strike the ground at high angles of elevation. This demanded a balancing spring, and it was very ingeniously fitted between the axle-tree and the end of the cradle; this spring in tension balanced the weight of the barrel. There was a small shield. The only drawback was the length of the trail legs, which tended to make the gun very trail-heavy when being manhandled; one man of the detachment usually draped himself across the muzzle, while the remainder lifted the trail to hook it to the towing vehicle.

DATA (Gun M2A1 on Carriage M2A2)

Calibre	105mm (4.13in)
Weight of gun and breech	1,064lb (483kg)
Total weight in action	4,980lb (2,259kg)
Barrel length	101.44in (2.58m)
Rifling	34 grooves, right-hand twist, one turn in 20 calibres
Recoil system and length	Hydro-pneumatic, constant, 42in (1,066mm)
Breech mechanism	Horizontal sliding block, manual; percussion firing
Elevation	-4 degrees 45' to +66 degrees 13'
Traverse	23 degrees right and left of zero
Shell weight	33lb (14.96kg)
Muzzle velocity	1,550ft/sec (472m/sec), Charge 7
Maximum range	12,205 yards (11,160m)
Types of projectile available	HE; HEAT; WP Smoke, BE Smoke, BE coloured smoke, chemical, canister

105mm Howitzer M2A1 continued

Practice firing with the 105mm howitzer M2A1 in 1942

Air Portability

In 1941, the US Army was looking to set up an airborne formation and asked for a 105mm howitzer which could be carried in the C-47 'Dakota' aircraft. A maximum weight of 2,500lb (1,136.35kg) and a range not less than 7,000 yards (6,420m) were the only guidelines.

The M2A1 howitzer barrel was cut down by 27in, with the breech being left exactly as it was; this allowed the firing of the standard 105mm ammunition, but with a specially reduced five-zone charge with smaller powder grains, so that the powder would be entirely consumed inside the short barrel. An ingenious designer realized that the near-redundant M3 75mm howitzer carriage could easily be modified and that the recoil system of the

75mm M8 howitzer carriage, suitably beefed up, would join the two together. Thus, the 105mm Howitzer M3 on Carriage M3 was born. The conversion was a little weak in spots, and a fresh design, with new, stronger, trail legs, appeared as the Carriage M3A1.

Although it was produced with air portability in mind, other divisions of the US Army viewed the M3 covetously. In 1941-42, the idea of 'Infantry Cannon Companies' provoked interest in various quarters of the US Army, and the M3 looked to be the very weapon for these companies. It was given a shield, turning the carriage into the M3A2, and a number of companies were formed. They were used in the North African campaign of 1942-43, but the idea was not a success; the infantry had enough

The real thing. Firing a 105mm howitzer in France, 1944

to do without trying to run their own artillery as well. The companies were disbanded in 1943, the shields removed, and the M3 remained a solely airborne equipment thereafter. It was made obsolete shortly after the war ended.

A Medium Field Gun

The last recommendation of the Westervelt Board relevant to this chapter was its demand for a medium field gun somewhere between the 105mm and 155mm calibres. The US Army did have a 4.7in field gun in small numbers during the First World War, and it was felt that this was a good calibre, so a new design was begun in 1920. The 4.7in Gun M1920 on Carriage, 4.7in Gun and 155mm Howitzer M1920 duly appeared; it was a split-trail design, but was unsatisfactory, and was replaced by Gun M1922E on Carriage M1921E. This 42-calibre gun, firing a 50lb (22.6kg) shell to a maximum range of 20,500 yards (18,810m), was considered suitable and was recommended for standardization. The formal decision was postponed for some small modifications to be made, but in August 1928 the whole project was

placed 'in abeyance' for the usual reason – shortage of money.

In 1939, the design was brought out again and examined, with a view to making some changes, to arrive at a gun firing to 20,000 yards (18,350m) and a carriage built from as many parts of the 155mm Howitzer M1 carriage as possible. A design was drawn up and was recommended for standardization in early 1940. At this point there was a strange and interesting occurrence.

In 1939, the British Army had decided upon a 4.5in gun to fit on the same carriage as the 5.5in medium gun, the idea being to replace the 60-pounder. In some unrecorded way – there is no mention of it in the Proceedings of the Ordnance Board – the British and the Americans got together and came to the conclusion that, sooner or later, they were likely to find themselves fighting side by side. In such a case, a measure of compatibility in armament would be useful. The American 4.7in gun was re-designed into 4.5in calibre, to suit the British 4.5in BL gun ammunition, and the Americans were furnished with ammunition manufacturing drawings. At the same time, arrangements were made for the manufacture of

The 105mm howitzer M3 was a shortened barrel on the carriage of the 75mm howitzer M2, seen here in France in 1944

some of the American ammunition in Canada. In April 1941, the 4.5in Gun M1 on Carriage M1 was standardized.

The carriage was almost the same as that of the 155mm Howitzer M1, described elsewhere. It had 65 degrees elevation, 53 degrees traverse and fired a 55lb (25kg) shell to 21,125 yards (19,380m) range.

The gun served throughout the war, largely as a training weapon, although a few were used in north-west Europe in 1944-45. Its principal drawback, according to the Americans, was the shell, which, by their standards was inefficient; like all British wartime shells, it was designed to use 19-ton steel and carried only 4½lb (2kg) of TNT. Americans preferred 23-ton steel, which gave thinner walls and more explosive capacity, but the number of guns in service did not justify setting up new manufacturing facilities. As a result, the gun was declared obsolete in September 1945.

RUSSIA

When Russia excused itself from the war in 1917, its artillery was a ragbag of weapons from a variety of sources – locally manufactured, license-built French and German, imported French, German and British. In the Russians' favour was the fact that the poor and ancient designs had all been weeded out by war; those that remained were good, sound pieces of equipment. This was just as well, because it was destined to serve the Russians through their own civil war, and well into the 1920s, before any thought could be given to replacing it.

The first piece of new equipment to be designed under the Communist regime came in 1927, a 76.2mm infantry-accompanying gun of simple and robust design which was manufactured by the thousand. A box-trail two-wheeled gun with shield, it fired a 6.2kg shell to a range of 8,550m. It was widely used during the war, and hundreds were

US airborne troops loading a 105mm howitzer M3 into a glider

The American 4.5in gun was on the same carriage as the 155mm howitzer and designed to fire British ammunition

captured by the Germans, who promptly assimilated them into their own infantry and even found it profitable to manufacture ammunition for them in Germany.

Re-Designs of 1930

The successful design of this little gun proved the credentials of the Soviet artillery design bureau. In 1930, they began to overhaul the surviving wartime weapons and bring them up to date by improving their carriages and developing better ammunition. These weapons can be recognized by their nomenclature, with the original year of design followed by the year of re-design: for example, the Divisional Gun M02/30.

The Divisional Gun M02/30 had begun life just after the Russo-Japanese War; designed by the Putilov factory, it fired a 6.6kg shell to 6,600m range. In common with most field guns of that period, it had a maximum elevation of only 17 degrees, and the barrel was 30 calibres long. The 1930 overhaul increased the elevation to 37 degrees, put a 40-calibre barrel on it, added a shield, and came up with a gun firing a 6.4kg shell to a range of 13,000m, almost double its original range.

The partner to this weapon was the 122mm

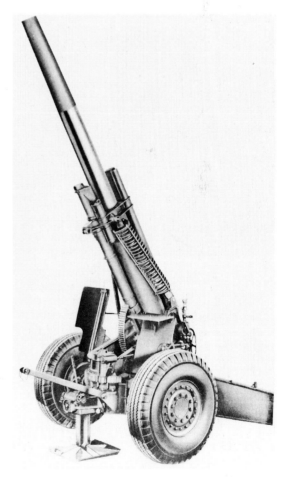

The 4.5in gun at maximum elevation, showing the firing pedestal which relieved the tyres of the firing shock

howitzer M10/30; originally a Schneider design purchased from France in some numbers, and thereafter built in various Russian factories, it had fired a 23kg shell to 7,690m range. In this instance, the designers were unable to give the weapon more elevation without excessive re-design, so they merely strengthened the carriage and overhauled the ammunition. This provided a more powerful propelling charge, so that, in the 10/30 form, it fired a 21.8kg shell to 8,900m. It was not so spectacular an improvement as that performed on the field gun, but quite a satisfactory gain for relatively little expense.

A similar improvement was performed on the 122mm 1908 howitzer, originally a Krupp design. Its performance was similar to that of the Schneider of 1910; it was given a similar treatment, strengthening the carriage and boosting the ammunition, and, in its 08/30 form, had exactly the same performance as the 10/30 howitzer.

Similar improvements were made to heavier guns, but for the time being the 1930 improved models formed the backbone of the Soviet Army's artillery. The designers were then put to work to produce fresh designs that would out-perform and eventually replace the 1930 school.

The M1936 and the M1939

The first new design to appear was still linked to the past; the 76.2mm Divisional Gun M1933 was a completely new 50-calibre gun inserted into the carriage of the 122mm M10/30 howitzer. This, being much stronger than the normal 76mm gun carriage, allowed the gun to be more powerful, and the end result was a weapon firing the standard 6.4kg 76mm shell to a range of 13,600 yards (12,480m) and having 43 degrees of elevation.

This change seemed to prove a point about the gun, and the next step was to design a completely new split tubular trail two-wheeled carriage with shield. A few minor changes were also made to the gun, which lengthened it to 51 calibres, and the result was called the 76mm Divisional Gun M1936. It had exactly the same performance as the M1933,

but the carriage was more modern, using rubber-tyred steel wheels instead of wooden, and was thus in tune with the on-going mechanization process sweeping through the Soviet Army. It also had a maximum elevation of 75 degrees, in a Soviet attempt to field an all-purpose gun: the extra elevation was supposed to allow it to fire in the anti-aircraft role. By 1938, virtually all the M1933 guns had been replaced by the M1936 design, which was mass-produced by several factories.

Like everybody else, the Soviets soon came to realize that 'all-purpose' guns were actually no-purpose guns, and the secondary role of the M1936 was quietly forgotten. However, one thing had made itself obvious in their attempts at vertical firing – continuous fire of the sort demanded by the air-defence role led to serious over-heating of the recoil system. The designers went back to the drawing board, and this time got it exactly right.

The 76mm Divisional Gun M1939 was new from top to bottom. The gun was of 41 calibres, and was carried in a cradle which had the recoil and recuperator cylinders above and below the barrel, where they were adequately cooled. The split-trail carriage generally followed the design of the 1933 model, but restricted the elevation to 42 degrees, with 57 degrees of traverse. In the interest of reducing bore wear, the charge was slightly reduced, so that the 6.4kg shell now went to a maximum range of 13,300m. One important feature was that the overall weight was brought down to 1,484kg (3,270lb), so that it was relatively easy to manhandle.

The M1941

The M1936 and the M1939 were the divisional artillery guns with which the Soviets met the Germans in 1941. They proved to be efficient and effective, but losses were in the thousands; the Germans took the M1936 and M1939 guns into their own service, as anti-tank guns. Production of guns was stepped up, and the designers looked hard at what they had in order to find some expeditious way of providing even more guns. One method was

The 76mm Infantry Gun M1927, the first gun design to appear after the Russian Revolution

to use bits and pieces already in volume production; in this way, the next 76mm gun, the M1941, was born.

The M1941 was the M1939 gun, with a muzzle brake added, fitted into the carriage of the 57mm anti-tank gun. The anti-tank carriage had been built with ample strength, to withstand the violent recoil, and it could easily accept the somewhat lesser force of the field piece, especially when damped down by a muzzle brake. Another benefit was that the weight came down to just over 1,100kg. It proved successful, but in practice it was found that the 57mm carriage was not quite as strong as the designers had thought; and, because it was an anti-tank carriage, the maximum elevation available to the gun was only 18 degrees, restricting the maximum range to about 11,000m. A new carriage, re-designed to provide additional strength without increasing the weight by more than a few kilos, and

with more elevation on the gun, was produced; the result was the 76mm Divisional Gun M1942, which restored the maximum range to 13,300m.

Field Guns as Anti-Tank Guns

This group of 76mm guns did valiant work in 1941–43, and continued in service throughout the war and for many years afterward. However, by the end of 1942, it was seen that the 76mm gun was no longer the ideal choice; the shell was simply not big enough to make an impression. Henceforth, the 122mm weapons would represent the bulk of the supporting artillery.

In their search for long range, using long barrels, and powerful charges fired from guns with split-trails and wide traverse, the Soviets had, unwittingly, provided themselves with several thousand potential anti-tank guns. By late 1942, it

The Russian 76.2mm Divisional Gun M1939; this had been captured by the Germans, fitted with a German muzzle brake, and taken into use as the 'Panzerabwehrkanone 39 (r)' anti-tank gun; it was then, as seen here, captured by US troops in Tunisia in 1942

was obvious that anti-tank guns were a vital necessity, and a new strategy was introduced. Shooting at tanks was no longer the sole prerogative of the anti-tank gunners' union. Anybody who saw a tank was required to shoot at it. Anti-tank ammunition was issued to all Soviet artillery capable of firing at zero elevation, but mostly to the 76mm guns, which were now primarily anti-tank guns, and secondarily field guns. The M1942 was issued with an armour-piercing shell, which would defeat 64mm of armour at 1,000m, a shaped charge shell capable of holing 70mm of armour at any range, and, later, a tungsten-cored arrowhead shot that could defeat 95mm of armour at 500m.

Two further field guns were developed during the war years – the 85mm Divisional Guns M1943 and

M1945 – but, like the 76mm guns, they became primarily anti-tank weapons. The Russians had introduced an 85mm gun in 1902, but it appears not to have been very successful and was obsolete by 1914. However, the calibre had its attractions – principally, a good combination of shell weight, range and gun weight – and, in terms of the anti-tank role, the idea made sense, because the barrel of the 85mm AA gun M1939 was already being adapted to use as a tank gun. It was now co-opted into a split-trail carriage based on that of the 76mm M1942. This produced the 85mm M1943, which could fire a 9.5kg shell to 16,600m (15,230 yards), an AP/HE shell to defeat 91mm of armour at 500m, or an arrowhead shot to defeat 113mm of plate at the same range.

7.62mm Divisional Gun M1942

The 3in field gun had been the standard divisional support gun of the Russian armies since the model of 1900, and the list of replacements is long and complicated, as designers strove for perfection. The wartime guns began with the M1936, which was probably the last appearance of the 'dual-purpose' weapon, since it had the ability to reach 75 degrees of elevation, and was intended to function as a forward-area anti-aircraft gun. This idea was soon seen to be useless, and the next attempt was the Model 1939, which could reach 45 degrees of elevation, and also split the recoil system above and below the barrel. Both these guns were produced in some numbers and put to use in the war, and both were captured by the Germans and modified into very useful anti-tank guns.

Next came the Model 1941, which used the 1939 gun on a light girder split-trail carriage, which it shared with the 57mm anti-tank guns. This proved to be too light and very few were made (of either gun) before a replacement came along – the Model 39/42, the M1939 gun on another split-trail carriage. Again, it was not a success, and the designers now produced a split-trail carriage with tubular trails, which was strong enough to stand up to the conditions on the Eastern Front. The carriage was adopted by the 57mm anti-tank gun, and the barrel of the M1939 76.2mm gun was placed upon it, to form the M1942 divisional gun.

The equipment was designed by the V.R.Grabin Design Bureau in Artillery Arsenal No. 2 in Gorky, and this time they had got it right; the result was an outstanding field and anti-tank gun, which was produced in vast numbers. It was to remain in service with Warsaw Pact countries well into the 1970s, and is still in use in several African and Eastern countries. The gun was also used in the T34 medium tank and, after the war, in the PT-76 amphibious tank.

The 76mm Divisional Gun M1942, with Russian muzzle brake, here on display at Aberdeen Proving Ground, USA

7.62mm Divisional Gun M1942 continued

DATA

Calibre	76.2mm (3.00in)
Weight of gun and breech	c. 620kg (1,366lb)
Total weight in action	1,200kg (2,646lb)
Barrel length	2.983m (117.45in)
Rifling	32 grooves, right-hand, one turn in 25 calibres
Recoil system and length	Hydro-pneumatic, variable, 673mm to 750mm (26.5 to 29.5in)
Breech mechanism	Vertical sliding block, semi-automatic; percussion firing
Elevation	- 5 degrees to + 37 degrees
Traverse	27 degrees right and left of zero
Shell weight	6.20kg (13.67lb)
Muzzle velocity	680m/sec (2,230ft/sec)
Maximum range	13,290m (12,152 yards)
Types of projectile available	HE; WP Smoke; shrapnel; incendiary, AP/HE, HEAT; HVAP Shot
Anti-armour performance	AP Shot: 69/500/0 : 61/1000/0; HVAP Shot: 92/500/0 : 58/1000/0; HEAT shell: 120mm at all ranges

---

As the anti-tank role gradually became more important than the field role, the M1943 was slightly re-designed. In its original form, it had 40 degrees of elevation; by cutting this down to 35 degrees, the gun could have a somewhat lower silhouette. This became the 85mm M1945 gun; it had the same anti-armour performance, but the maximum range with an HE shell was reduced to 15,500m.

122mm Weapons

The place of the field gun was now taken by the 122mm group of weapons. This calibre (48 lines in old Russian measure, 4.8in, and actually 121.9mm in practice) has been a peculiarly Russian calibre since the late nineteenth century, and the first 'modern' weapon was a 1904 howitzer. Prior to the First World War, Krupp and Schneider howitzers were bought in this calibre; they had actually been designed by their makers in 120mm, but were bored out and re-rifled to suit the Russians. One of the Russian designers' first tasks in their 1930s overhaul was to update two of the old-pattern howitzers.

M1938

Once that was done, the next job was to produce a modern replacement, and this appeared as the 122mm Howitzer M1938. This weapon must, surely, be the most prolific piece of artillery in history. It was produced continuously from 1938 until well into the 1960s, was the principal divisional artillery weapon of the Soviet Army and the Warsaw Pact armies, and was supplied by the thousand to anyone who could raise the price, anywhere in the world. There are hundreds of them still in use, and it will be well into the twenty-first century before the last of them goes to the scrapyard.

The M1938 howitzer was approved in September 1938 and began reaching troops in the summer of 1939. It was designed by the F.F. Petrov Bureau of Artillery Factory No. 172 at Perm; construction began at Perm and soon spread to a number of other factories. It was issued on a generous scale: thirty-six to a Motorized Rifle Division in two battalions each of three batteries with six guns, and fifty-four to a Tank Division in three battalions. It was a simple and robust design

The 122mm Howitzer M1942, showing the spring suspension and the lower ends of the spring balancing units

of split-trail two-wheeled carriage with shield, the gun moving in a ring cradle, with the recoil buffer below and the recuperator above. As with most Soviet guns of its era, the tyres were rubber, filled with sponge rubber, fitted to disc wheels; this system has continued to the present day. Post-war licence-built Bulgarian and Chinese howitzers use the same type of tyres.

The M1938 fired a 21.7kg (47.8lb) shell to a range of 11,800m (12,900 yards), and is remarkable in that its performance is still exactly the same; no improvements to ammunition or any other feature have been made in an attempt to extract more range from it. Another unusual point is that it is possible, and permissible, to fire the howitzer without opening the trail legs, the only drawback being that the available traverse is severely limited to 1.5 degrees. It was originally provided with the usual options of high explosive and smoke shells, and these were augmented by shrapnel and illuminating projectiles, and, in late 1942, by a shaped charge anti-tank shell capable of penetrating 100mm of armour.

M1931

Although most of the 1930 weapons were make-overs of pre-1914 designs, one new design appeared at this time, filling what the Soviet Army saw as a gap in their armoury. They had no long-

ranging divisional gun, so the design bureau produced the 122mm M1931 gun, a weapon to fire a 25kg shell to 20,875m (22,755 yards) – no mean performance for that period. A split-trail carriage with two spoked, solid-tyred wheels, it carried the gun in a trough cradle which extended well behind the breech in a manner reminiscent of the Schneider howitzers. Perhaps the most obvious feature was the two vertical balancing spring cylinders in front of the shield, supporting the cradle and barrel weight. This seems to be the first application of this method of balancing the barrel weight, and it spread rapidly to several countries during the next few years.

M1931/37

The 1938 howitzer shared its carriage with a 152mm weapon, and this form of rationalization was extended with the design of the next 122mm gun, the M1931/37, often described as a gun-howitzer. The same barrel as the M1931 was now adapted to a carriage designed to carry either it or a 152mm gun-howitzer; at a casual glance there appears to be no difference between the M1931 and early M1931/37 models, but very soon the 31/37 was given dual rubber-tyred disc wheels. It also has a tubular strut on top of the folded trail, to which the gun breech ring can be locked when it is pulled back in its cradle into the travelling position. The

Soviet troops at practice with the 122mm howitzer M1942

M1931 had a maximum elevation of 45 degrees, but the 31/37 increased this to 65 degrees, to give it a howitzer capability; the weight of shell and maximum range remained the same.

107mm Weapons

Soviet field artillery also included two minority groups. The first of these was another peculiarly Russian calibre – 107mm (42 lines or 4.2in) – which had been adopted in the 1870s. In the early 1900s, two new guns, one from Krupp and one from Schneider, both originally designed as 105mm pieces, were purchased in relatively small numbers. In 1930, the surviving Schneider guns were given a new longer barrel, to be re-modelled into the 107mm Gun M1910/30. This allowed them to fire a 17.2kg (38lb) shell to a range of 16,350m (17,880 yards). (The remaining Krupp weapons appear to have been disposed of to the Spanish Republicans during the Spanish Civil War.)

A new 107mm design was called for in the late 1930s, resulting in the 107mm Gun M1940. This was an all-new design with a 43.5-calibre barrel on a split-trail carriage with pneumatic tyres and a new recoil system, probably that of the 122mm Howitzer M1938 suitably modified. It fired the same 17.2kg shell to a range of 17,450m (19,000 yards). Very few were built; there is a number of theories as to why this was the case. One is that the initial German advances in 1941 over-ran the factory where production was just getting into its stride; another is that it was decided to concentrate on the 122mm calibre as standard, and reduce the number of calibres in service; a third, that the army had second thoughts, considered it too much gun for too small a shell, and decided that the 122mm represented a better combination. Each of these theories seems logical, and the decision may have been the result of a combination of all three. Whatever the explanation, the 107mm M1940 vanished in 1941.

Mountain Guns

The second minority group was the mountain guns. Pre-1914 Russia was always liable to drop everything in order to have at the Turks if the opportunity arose; the Russo-Turkish border was largely mountainous, so the Russians' stock of mountain artillery was quite extensive. In the post-1919 period, the need was somewhat less, but numbers of these guns were retained. By 1935, they were feeling their age, and in 1936 the Soviets purchased a small number of 75mm M36 mountain guns from Skoda of Czechoslovakia. Using these as their prototype, the Soviets enlarged the bore to suit their 76.2mm standard, and then put the gun into production as the 76.2mm mountain gun M1938.

A box-trail carriage with pneumatic-tyred wheels and a shield carried the short 23-calibre barrel in a prominent jacket over a tubular recoil system. As with all mountain guns, the M1938 came to pieces for mule transport, or could be towed by horses or trucks. It fired a 6kg (13.2lb) shell to a range of 10,100m (11,050 yards), offering quite good performance for a mountain gun. It had a maximum elevation of 70 degrees, so that it could function as a howitzer, and the all-up weight was only 795kg (1,750lb).

3 Medium and Heavy Artillery

HEAVY ARTILLERY OR THE BOMBER?

Heavy artillery was in an invidious position in the between-wars years. On the one hand, the introduction of motor traction, which put an end to weight restrictions, led to the promise of bigger and better guns and howitzers. On the other hand, the advocates of aviation were certain that heavy artillery was now obsolete, the task of demolishing the enemy's rear areas having been taken over by the bomber.

The arguments bothered planners and strategists and, with the continuing shortage of finance, many were happy to accept the assurances of the aviators. They were inclined to put heavy-artillery considerations aside, and spend the available cash on other forms of weaponry. It seemed a logical decision, given the conditions of the time. However, the designers and armaments manufacturers were not convinced. Motor traction was measurable, and could be assessed and tested. Aviation was a promise, not yet capable of being proven in practice. When they were off duty, the designers continued with heavy-artillery designs, seeking ways to move the largest calibres by mechanical means. As it turned out, this was just as well. Germany, the one nation who had the right idea about aviation support for their ground forces, and regarded the *Stuka* dive-bomber and Dornier light bomber as extensions of the army's artillery, never faltered in its dedication to heavy artillery and produced a number of heavy guns which were long-ranging and highly mobile. Had Allied designers not beavered away in their off-time

between 1920 and 1935, things might have looked very different in 1939–45.

SUPER-GUNS

The extremes of giantism, explored by the Germans, were left virtually untouched by the Allies. They had been suitably impressed by Big Bertha in 1914 and the Paris Gun in 1918, and there had been a brief flurry of paper ideas for super-guns in 1919–20. Vickers actually lined a 16in gun down to 8in calibre, 104 calibres long, and fired it at their Eskmeals range in February 1919, using a 282lb (128kg) cordite charge. The shell reached a velocity of 4,400ft/sec (1,340m/sec) but there is no record of what range was achieved. The barrel displayed a 102in longitudinal split after the sixth round and that was the end of the enterprise.

The enthusiasm soon passed, and in the colder climate of the years that followed, the super-gun proposition was clinically dissected. Capital expenditure, manufacturing man-hours, weight of shell, weight of payload and probable error were all considered. The conclusion reached was that super-weapons were good only for propaganda purposes, being insufficiently accurate or damaging, prone to wear out rather quickly, and unbearably expensive.

Despite this, the British *did* build a super-gun – however, it was not a successful story.

SE170 and SE171

The Director of Naval Ordnance began the story in 1940, with a suggestion to develop a long-range

A 6in Mark XIX gun of 65 Medium Regiment in action in France, 1940. Of a First World War design, most were left behind at Dunkirk, with only a handful remaining in the Middle East and in Britain, for training purposes

gun for army use. The army was less enthusiastic, seeing no tactical employment for it under modern warfare conditions. DNO pressed for it on the grounds that, even if the army did not need it now, they might in the future and, in any case, it would be a valuable ballistic experimental tool. At that time, no specific calibre or size was stated, but eventually an 8in of 140 calibres was suggested, firing a 256lb (116.12kg) shell at 5,500ft/sec (1,676m/sec).

The immediate objection to this was that there was then no gun lathe in the country capable of turning a barrel of 93ft 4in (28.45m); the answer was to suggest that the rifled portion of the barrel be made in two pieces. The objection to this was that a two-piece construction would not withstand the high pressures and velocities that were foreseen. The idea was not pursued.

Finally, it was decided to use an 8in 90-calibre (60 ft/18.3m) inner tube (the longest piece that could be made on existing machinery), fitted into a 13.5in Mark 5 gun body, the 13.5in breech being modified to suit the rear of the 8in chamber. Two guns were made – SE170 and SE171 – by Vickers-Armstrong, and a mounting was made by the Great Western Railway workshops at Swindon, based

upon a naval 13.5in warship barbette mounting.

The mounting, carrying the first gun, SE170, was installed in late 1942 at Yantlet Battery on the Isle of Grain in the Thames Estuary. (This was an experimental site on the north shore of the island, used by the Proof & Experimental Establishment at Shoeburyness, on the north side of the estuary, when they needed to do long-range firing.) A few experimental shots were fired; this showed that this location was of little use, because the range of the gun sent the shells well past the observed ranges off Shoeburyness, where the fall of shot could be measured. A second location had to be found, and eventually a location just north of Dover was selected. SE170 was removed, the mounting was sent down to Dover and re-assembled, and Gun SE171 was fitted to it.

It seems probable that there were thoughts about directing this gun towards German-occupied France, with particular emphasis on some of the German cross-channel batteries. The gun, now christened 'Bruce' (after Admiral Sir Bruce Fraser, Controller of the Navy), was manned by a Royal Marine Siege Battery. The *Proceedings of the Ordnance Board* takes up the tale:

Firing was carried out on 30 and 31 March and 2 April 1943. Gun No SE171, on 13.5in Barbette Carriage Mk II* No 27 at Royal Marine Siege Battery, Dover.

Shells of three types were fired, all fitted with Fuze No 241. Propelling charge Cordite SC/S weight 247lb. Maximum range observed was 96,659 yards achieved at 42 degrees 52' quadrant elevation. Time of flight 145.89 seconds.

One round was unobserved and heard to fall at approximately 100,000 yards range. Muzzle velocity varied between 4,500ft/sec and 4,573ft/sec. 22 rounds were fired. Height to vertex of trajectory 84,100 feet (25,637m). Mean deviation in each series of shots was 0.4 per cent of range. 50 per cent breadth zone at maximum range about 75 yards.

Some rounds burst in the air, and the board requests the Chief Engineer, Armaments Design (CEAD) to put forward a fresh design of shell modified for a fuze of the 118 type, a design with a fuze inside the ballistic cap, and a base fuze. A probable barrel life of twenty-eight effective full charge rounds appears to be indicated from the wear figures reported.

No high priority was given to the manufacture of special projectiles (they were ribbed, the gun having sixteen very deep rifling grooves), and the next firing took place on 20 September 1944:

Commanding Officer RM Siege Regiment reports on the firing of shells fitted with modified No 118 fuzes from the 13.5/8in gun. One shell burst at 61,150 yards range and 60,000 feet height, and one burst only 1,500 yards from the gun. It is believed to be a heat effect, and it is proposed to insulate the fuze from the explosive filling by means of asbestos and, as an alternative solution, abandon the use of a fuze and use a ballistic cap with stick actuation of a gaine fitted in the shell nose.

'Bruce' never featured in the *Proceedings* again, and the project was closed down very shortly afterwards. According to legend, the RM pointed it in the general direction of Germany one day and

This Vickers 9.2in howitzer was proposed as a replacement for the old pattern, but was abandoned in favour of the American 240mm howitzer

loosed off a couple of rounds; unfortunately, there is probably little truth in that story. About fifteen years later, I tripped over the SE171 barrel one day when walking through the long grass of the gun compound at Shoeburyness. I believe it finally went to the scrapyard during the immense spring-cleaning which took place when the future London Airport was being planned on Maplin Sands in the 1960s.

DISPOSITION OF HEAVY ARTILLERY

Broadly, the disposition of heavy artillery was similar in most armies. Guns and howitzers in the 6in/155mm class were sometimes part of the divisional artillery, but many regiments, and anything above that calibre, would be classed as 'GHQ Artillery', or Corps or Army artillery, and would be under the hand of the artillery commander of the particular higher formation. He would then attach batteries or regiments of heavy weapons to divisions for specific operations where the particular type of weapon was appropriate. Once the operation was concluded, the units would return to the higher formation and await their next task. Sometimes, the 'operation' lasted a long time; for example, some British heavy regiments were attached to divisions at the start of the Italian campaign, and remained with them for the rest of the war.

BRITAIN

Britain ended the war in 1918 with a huge armoury of heavy guns and howitzers, brought into being by the conditions particular to trench warfare. Much of it was rapidly scrapped, leaving only the most modern examples of the 8in, 9.2in and 12in howitzers and 6in guns in service. 'Most modern' is a relative term; in this case, it means 'those of the latest manufacturing date'. There was very little that was 'modern' about the 8in howitzers, for example; they were short-barrelled weapons on simple box-trails, with massive 'traction-engine' wheels. Their recoil systems were so ineffective that it was necessary to place ramps behind the wheels; on firing, the carriage recoiled up the ramp and then rumbled down again into the firing position (or fairly close to it).

As a result, heavy artillery needed to be considered in the late 1920s. However, with the Royal Air Force's assurance that it could take over the artillery's job and deliver bombs on whatever targets were pointed out, the gun designers turned to other work – including a new anti-aircraft gun, and the defence of Singapore.

A 5.5in Gun

Another thing that needed to be addressed was a replacement for the ageing 60-pr (5in) gun as the medium support weapon. After much discussion, in

Another British proposal was this 6in gun, but the American 155mm gun M1 elbowed it aside before development had been completed

Ordnance, 5.5in Gun Mark 3 on Carriage Marks 1 or 2

In January 1939, an Operational Requirement called for a new 5in calibre gun firing a 90lb shell to 16,000 yards, and weighing less than 5.5 tons. The ballistic experts studied this for a while and reported back that a better solution would be a 5.5in gun, firing a 100lb shell; the 5.5in gun came into being.

The designers set to work with great enthusiasm. No expense was spared to incorporate all the most recent ideas, but the result turned out to be rather less than the sum of the various parts, and some of the ideas had to be designed out again. The gun was to be an autofrettaged barrel in a loose jacket, with an Asbury screw breech mechanism. This was unexceptional, but it was given a 'Lock, Percussion L in Slide Box AC' as the firing mechanism. This complicated semi-automatic device was difficult to dismantle for cleaning, and showed a number of ways of going wrong. The mechanism had originally been designed for use in the clean environment of naval turret guns, where it had performed quite reliably, but the mud and dust of field service were too much for it. In 1941, it was removed and replaced by the 'Lock, Percussion, K, and Slide Box Y', a much simpler mechanism, which had been first put into service in 1917.

The carriage was an up-to-date split-trail type with two wheels and with the gun in a trough cradle, which was trunnioned well back and balanced by means of a pair of complex hydro-pneumatic rams carried vertically to lift the cradle. These proved to be a fertile source of trouble, prone to leak; if one leaked more than the other, it tended to twist the cradle and damage the recoil system. They were difficult and expensive to manufacture, difficult to adjust and maintain, and eventually were discarded and replaced by a much simpler spring design. These were fitted in the same manner, and gave the gun its distinctive appearance, the two balancing spring cylinders rising like a pair of horns.

There was also a quick-loading gear, which gave no trouble. This was a very simple but ingenious design, which unlocked the cradle from the elevating arc and allowed the gun to be swung down to the horizontal for loading while the gun-layer was still busy setting the elevation and traverse. Once loaded, all hands bore down on the end of the cradle, and the gun barrel swung up until the lock snapped into place in the elevating arc, and the gun was at the proper elevation. This was much quicker and easier than winding it up and down between each shot.

Once the gun got into service, in May 1942, it rapidly became popular, and, apart from a spell of premature explosions in the barrel in Italy (eventually traced to carelessness with the ammunition allied with worn barrels), it gave sterling service throughout the war and for many years afterwards. It was finally declared obsolete in the 1980s. It is still in use in South Africa where, with modern ammunition, it reaches a maximum range of 21,000m.

DATA (Mark 3 gun on Mark 2 carriage)

Calibre	5.5in (139.7mm)
Weight of gun and breech	4,120lb (1,869kg)
Total weight in action	13,646lb (6,190kg)
Barrel length	171.6in (4.358m)
Rifling	36 grooves, right-hand twist, one turn in 20 calibre
Recoil system and length	Hydro-pneumatic, variable, 30 to 54in (762 to 1,371mm)
Breech mechanism	Asbury with Welin screw, percussion firing
Elevation	30 degrees each side of zero
Shell weight	100lb (45.36kg); 80lb (36.28kg)
Muzzle velocity	1,675ft/sec (510m/sec) with 100lb shell (Ch 4) 1,950ft/sec (594m/sec) with 80lb shell (Ch Super)
Maximum range	16,200 yds (14,813m) with 100lb shell; 18,100 yds (16,550m) with 80lb shell
Types of projectile available	HE; BE smoke, BE coloured smoke; BE incendiary

Ordnance, 5.5in Gun Mark 3 on Carriage Marks 1 or 2 continued

The 5.5in gun in firing position; it must have been raining – somebody has put the muzzle cover over the dial sight

January 1939 a new 5in gun was requested, to fire a 90lb (41kg) shell to 16,000 yards (14,680m), and weigh not more than 5½ tons. The subsequent ballistic calculations showed that a better solution would be a shell of 5.5in calibre, so the plans were re-drawn and the 5.5in gun came into existence. It was a split-trail carriage weapon, with two distinctive 'horns' in front of the trunnions, which contained the balancing springs.

As noted elsewhere, the designers were too ambitious and this led to delays in manufacturing the carriage, with the result that the gun was not ready for issue until May 1942, the first weapons going to North Africa. They proved to be successful and popular, in spite of a rash of premature detonations of the shell in the bore during the Italian campaign. These were eventually ascribed to an unfortunate combination of a number of small factors – including dirt, mud, and worn barrels – which had come together with disastrous effect. Once this was solved, the gun gave no more trouble. It was to stay in British service until the 1980s, and is still in service with the South African army.

The only objection which the army had to the 5.5 was a lack of range. Its maximum was 16,200 yards (14,860m); this had been asked for in the first instance, but things had moved on since then. An 82lb (37.25kg) shell (always referred to as an '80lb') was therefore designed and, with a new 'super' charge, this took the maximum range up to 18,100 yards (16,600m). The shell achieved its weight by having a finer taper and being made of a higher-grade steel, allowing thinner walls. The result was that the terminal effect was practically indistinguishable from that of the original 100lb (45kg) shell, so that eventually the 100lb was

Loading the 5.5in gun; the kneeling man in the foreground holds the cartridge and is waiting for the shell to be rammed before taking it to the breech

The open breech of the 5.5in gun, showing the three-stepped Welin breech screw, the central vent, and, at the extreme right, the handle of the firing lock

The 5.5in breech closed; the firing lock is also closed and the firing lanyard will be hooked into the ring at the bottom right of the lock

abandoned, to be entirely replaced by the 80lb.

The Lack of Heavy Artillery

In the summer of 1937, the heavy artillery question came up again. It had become obvious that the RAF was never likely to have sufficient aircraft to provide effective support for the field army, and that, even if they had, they appeared to have no inclination for the job. A new heavy gun and howitzer suddenly became very desirable. In April 1938, when the matter was finally debated, the decision was taken to draw up designs for a 7.85in

(200mm) howitzer firing a 300lb (136kg) shell to 16,000 yards (14,680m), and a 6.85in (174mm) gun firing a 100lb (45kg) shell to 26,500 yards (24,310m).

Before either of them were even designed, a fresh change of policy abandoned the 7.65in in favour of a new and more mobile 9.2in howitzer; and, just as war broke out, the 6.85in gun was also dropped. This meant that, as the Army set off to France in 1939, there was no modern heavy gun, even on paper. The 1st Heavy Regiment (the only one in existence) went across the Channel with twelve 8in howitzers and four 6in guns, which had been

An unusual picture of a 5.5in gun with shields, and with the original hydro-pneumatic balancing cylinders. The shields were never put into service

modernized to the extent of fitting pneumatic-tyred wheels. More heavy regiments were mobilized, but the supply of 8in howitzers and 6in guns ran out, and the cumbersome 9.2in howitzer was the only road-mobile armament available. Also, when the evacuation from Dunkirk took place, twelve 6in guns, twelve 8in howitzers and twenty-four 9.2in howitzers were among the 2,700 guns left behind in France.

The British Army therefore had virtually no heavy artillery, other than a small number of railway guns. The Royal Navy, as in the previous war, tried to rally round, producing a collection of obsolete naval guns from store. They were offered to the army, but this time the offer was declined on the grounds that 'these monster equipments' were likely to be a liability in modern fast-moving warfare.

The 7.2in Howitzer

In the wake of Dunkirk, one of the first things the General Staff asked for was a replacement for the 8in howitzer, something with longer range with which to counter-bombard enemy guns. In November 1940, a new weapon, the 7.2in howitzer, was approved. In fact, this was no more than the old

A medium regiment preparing for a major operation in Germany, 1945. This picture illustrates the reality of Allied air superiority; lining guns up wheel to wheel like this would be fatal if the enemy had air superiority

8in howitzer with a linered-down barrel, firing a new 200lb (91kg) shell. It still had the short box-trail, and still needed the 'quoins' or wedges behind the wheels to try to contain the recoil (which was now rather worse, due to a more powerful charge), but it could reach to 16,900 yards (15,505m), a 30 per cent improvement on the 8in howitzer. There were actually four different marks of 7.2, depending on which mark of 8in howitzer had been used for the conversion; the carriage was the same for all four.

These 7.2in howitzers saw service in North Africa and Italy, but experience showed that, when firing Charge 4, the weapon was almost uncontrollable. It needed too much adjustment and repositioning after each round to allow a reasonable rate of fire to be sustained, so, early in 1943, it was decided to design a new carriage.

At about this time, the American 155mm Gun M1 was arriving in Britain; the carriage was an excellent split-trail type, with an eight-wheel bogie, which could be lifted from the ground to lower the carriage body into firm contact and provide a very stable platform. Somebody pointed out that the Americans also mounted their 8in howitzer on the same carriage, so why not put the 7.2in on it as

well? The idea was accepted, and the combination of a 7.2in howitzer, Marks 1 to 4, and the American M1 carriage became the 7.2in Mark 5.

Few 7.2in Mark 5s were made, however; just as production was about to start, it was pointed out that allying a modern carriage with such an elderly lash-up as the 7.2in converted from the 8in was over-doing it. There was too much carriage for too little gun. It would make more sense to develop a completely new 7.2in howitzer to take advantage of the greater stability of the American carriage. As a result, a completely new howitzer was designed, built, tested, and approved in December 1943 as the Mark 6. It increased the maximum range by about two miles, to 19,600 yards (17,900 m) with the same 200lb (91kg) shell, largely by being able to fire a heavier charge of propellant.

The 9.2in Howitzer

The 9.2in howitzer had been introduced at the start of the war, in 1914, and an improved Mark 2 version appeared in 1916. This was a cumbersome piece of equipment, which had originally been designed to be dismantled into three major units – barrel, carriage body and cradle, and carriage bed –

Preparing ammunition for 9.2in howitzers during training on Salisbury Plain, 1942

each to be drawn by a team of horses. Traction was later done by Holt caterpillar tractors, but it was still a slow-moving item and took several hours of very hard work to assemble and put into action. One of the detachment's major worries was the need to fill an 'earth box' with 11 tons of soil, to keep the carriage from jumping into the air when the howitzer fired.

About a dozen of these were in existence in 1939, and five of them were left in France in 1940, three with a heavy regiment and two as reserves. The remainder were dispersed around southern England as anti-invasion weapons, covering likely landing beaches. They were obviously too slow to fit into a fast-moving war, and when their anti-invasion role was finished they were retired into store to await being made obsolete as soon as the war ended.

A New Vickers Design

In early 1939, a new design had been commissioned from Vickers-Armstrong and from Woolwich Arsenal. Wooden mock-ups were made, and the Vickers design was selected. A prototype was built and fired successfully in 1941. Handling and travelling trials and modifications took another year. The weapon used a split-trail carriage with a four-wheeled bogie and could fire a 315lb (143kg) shell to a range of 16,000 yards (14,630m). It could be brought into or out of action in half an hour, a considerable improvement on the 1916 design.

All seemed set for approval and production, but in October 1942, the project was abandoned. No reason has been found for this decision, but it is probable that the imminent supply of the 240mm (9.45in) howitzer M1 from the USA was the deciding factor. This weapon would be in production and could be ready for use long before production of the new 9.2 could be achieved.

The 12in Howitzer

The last major British super-heavy weapon was the 12in howitzer, which was simply the 9.2in enlarged. Being bigger, it was moved in six loads, drawn by Holt tractors or steam engines at little more than walking pace; it was nicknamed 'the twelve-inch road-hog'. Once emplaced, which could take half a day or more, it fired a 750lb (340kg) shell to a range of 14,350 yards (13,120m). Probably less than a dozen of these equipments existed in 1939, and they were all emplaced in the anti-invasion role in 1940. After that, they saw little use.

There was a proposal in 1943 to develop an anti-concrete shell and form the equipments into a super-heavy road regiment for the invasion of Europe. Their role was to be to batter their way through the defences of *Festung Europa*, but by this time the tactical air support question had been examined and refined, and there was very little point in labouring to bring one of these monsters into action when air power could do the same job. The anti-concrete shells were never made and the 12in howitzer received its obsoletion orders in March 1945.

USA

During the First World War, the US Army, having no heavy field guns of its own, adopted the French 155mm gun and howitzer, and the British 8in and 9.2in howitzers. Between the wars, the two 155mm equipments were the standards, while the two British equipments went into store; some of the 8ins were returned to Britain in 1940 to be converted into 7.2in howitzers. The remainder served as training guns until they could be replaced by modern weapons, after which they were withdrawn and scrapped.

The Westervelt Board Recommendations

The Westervelt Board had recommended the development of a 155mm gun capable of 65 degrees of elevation, all-round traverse, and a shell weighing about 100lb (45kg), which would be interchangeable with that of the 155mm howitzer. The range 'should be about 25,000 yards' and it should be rubber-tyred for motor traction at about 12mph. This was to be supplemented by an 8in howitzer using the same carriage, firing a 240lb (109kg) shell to about 18,000 yards (16,515m).

Regarding heavier weapons, the board suggested a gun of about 8in calibre, firing a 220lb (100kg) shell to 35,000 yards (32,110m), and a 9.5in howitzer, firing a shell not over 400lb (181.8kg) to a range of about 25,000 yards (22,935m). All these weapons were to be road-mobile, and in each case it

A British 12in Mark 4 howitzer in France, 1940

The 7.2in howitzer Mark 1 was simply a new barrel fitted on to the carriage of the old 8in howitzer

Controlling the recoil on the 7.2in howitzer Mark 1 was partly performed by a normal recoil system, but also by allowing the gun to recoil up these ramps or 'quoins', so as to soak up some of the energy

Firing a 7.2in howitzer in Italy, 1943; the carriage is half-way up the ramp and the barrel at full recoil in the cradle. The gun-layer, on the far side, is holding the dial sight; it was always removed before firing, in case it was jolted out of its socket. The object in front of the kneeling man is a loudspeaker connected to the command post and delivering fire orders to the gun

was proposed that a self-propelled mounting might be the best solution.

It is rare to read the recommendations of a board of this type and then, years later, look back and see that the system worked. What the Westervelt Board asked for, the US Army got. They may have had to wait twenty or more years for most of it, but the recommendations of the board were adhered to throughout that time. There were no second thoughts or revised opinions, the designers just kept working until they got the designs right, and then they were put into production just in time to win the next war.

The 7.2in howitzer Mark 6 was a new barrel mounted on the carriage of the American 8in how/155mm gun, giving a considerable increase in performance and a much more stable weapon

Firing the 7.2in howitzer Mark 6; the next round is lying on the loading tray, with the rammer, and the dial sight stays in its socket

Design Work Between the Wars

Work on designs to reflect the Westervelt Board's ideas began in 1920. It was frequently interrupted or slowed down by lack of finance in the 1925-35 period, but it continued – designs were drawn up, discussed and dissected, put back together again on paper, torn up, changed, re-done, and argued about until they were found satisfactory, then they were put away and another one was begun. In this way, the pitfalls of over-hasty production were avoided, and it is hard to find any serious defect in any of these between-wars designs.

The 155 mm GPF

The 155mm gun in use in 1918 was the French GPF (Grande Puissance, Filloux, or 'high power, designed by Filloux'), which was in US service as the M1917. This was a good design of split-trail two-wheeled carriage (the first large-calibre split-trail ever built), with a powerful gun, firing a 95lb (43kg) shell to 16,200 yards (14,860m) range. During the 1919–39 period, it was periodically improved by the Americans; the M1918 was the same gun but manufactured in the USA, and the carriage was given pneumatic tyres, roller bearings, electric brakes and, later, air brakes. The ammunition was improved, so that eventually the M1918 had a maximum range of 21,100 yards (19,355m).

Even though the GPF was, at that time, considered to be the best gun of its class in the world, the Westervelt Board had asked for 25,000 yards (22,935m), so the designers went to work. The 155mm M1920M1 appeared on a carriage similar to that of the GPF, but engineered to allow 65 degrees of elevation (instead of the 35 degrees of the GPF), and it reached 25,860 yards (23,725m) in trial firings. Work was then stopped for some time, but in 1929 it was revived and an entirely new gun and carriage design was begun. This was standardized as the 155mm Gun M1 in 1938. Production began in the following year and, by the time of the US entry into the war, sixty-five had been built.

The 155mm Gun M1 with the barrel retracted for travelling and secured to the trail by an A-frame. This is probably one of the pilot models, since there are some minor differences between it and the standard weapons

The 155mm Howitzer M1917

The 155mm howitzer M1917 was another French design adopted by the US Army. A simple and robust box-trail carriage carried the short barrel in an elongated cradle typical of Schneider's designs. It fired a 95lb (43kg) shell to a range of 11,500m (12,535 yards). As with the gun, the Americans first bought the howitzers from Schneider, built them in the USA, then made a few modifications and improved the ammunition; in this case, there was no improvement in performance, the maximum range staying the same. The carriage, by 1939, was equipped with pneumatic tyres and air brakes for high-speed towing. The M1917 and its American-built equivalent, the M1918, spent most of the Second World War as training weapons, although some use was made of them in the Far East and a number were sent to North Africa for use by the British until they had enough 5.5in guns.

The 155mm Howitzer M1

This relegation of the M1917 was due to its replacement in first-line service by a much-improved weapon, the 155mm howitzer M1. If the M1917 could be said to have a defect, it was the method of traversing the gun on its carriage. The axle was formed into a screw-thread; turning a captive nut attached to the carriage allowed the carriage to move sideways across the axle for 3 degrees in either direction. For changes of direction greater than this, the whole carriage had to be 'run up' to free the spade, then moved bodily – almost four tons in weight. During the 1920s, a number of

ground platforms were designed and tried, in the hope of finding a way of providing a greater arc of fire with as little labour as possible, but none were effective. In 1934, work therefore began on a completely new split-trail carriage, which would give 30 degrees of traverse and 65 degrees of elevation, permit a maximum range of 16,000 yards (14,680m) and have an all-up weight of under 11,000lb (5,000kg).

This work went along smoothly until 1939, when it occurred to somebody that there was little sense in designing a beautiful new carriage only to mount a howitzer of 1917 design on it. This brought the work to a stop, everything was torn up, and the drawing office got busy on a completely fresh equipment, new from muzzle to trail eye, with the proviso that the carriage should mount either a new 155mm howitzer or an equally new 4.7in gun. The ominous noises coming from Europe acted as a stimulant, the designers moved fast, and the new equipment was standardized as the 155mm Howitzer M1 in May 1941.

The carriage, it would seem, was more or less that which had been under development since 1934, since it had all the desired attributes of traverse, elevation and range, although it was a trifle over the stipulated weight. The howitzer was a new 20-calibre barrel with a better breech mechanism, and, to provide stability when firing, there was a firing pedestal in the centre of the axle, which could be lowered to the ground to take the weight off the wheels. It soon gained a reputation for phenomenal accuracy and consistency; just over six thousand were made during the war, and afterwards they were retained in service and widely

155mm Gun M2 on Carriage M1A1

The 155mm Gun M1 at maximum elevation

The American development of a new 155mm gun to replace the French M1917 began in 1920, because the Westervelt Board considered that a range of 25,000 yards ought to be available if the gun had sufficient elevation. Two guns were built: the M1920, which was a built-up gun of nickel steel, and the M1920M1, a wire-wound gun (probably the last of that type ever developed in the USA). A split-trail carriage giving 65 degrees elevation was also designed, with provision for removing the barrel and transporting it on a separate transport trailer. The magic 25,000 yards was reached, and the design was closed down and put to one side. The idea was revived in 1929 and a new gun, the T4, was begun, intended to be even more powerful. The Schneider breech of the M1917 and M1920 was abandoned, and a new Asbury-type mechanism, using a side lever, was designed. It went through various tests and modifications, emerging as the T4E2, and was standardized as the M1 in 1938.

At the same time, a completely new carriage, the T5, was developed. This was a masterpiece by any standards. It was a split-trail pattern, with the front end carried on a four dual-wheel bogie attached to the carriage body by two enormous screwed rods. Above this was a traversing top carriage carrying the cradle, recoil system and gun, trunnioned well back, and balanced by two hydro-pneumatic cylinders, which ran from the top of the top carriage to support the cradle. The trail ends were carried on a two-wheeled limber.

On going into action, the limber was removed, and the trail legs spread, holes were dug and the spades dropped in and pinned to the trail legs. Then, four men with two huge ratchet spanners turned the screwed rods until the carriage rested on the ground, and the wheels were suspended in the air. For travelling, the gun could be disconnected from the recoil system and pulled back in the cradle, the breech being supported on the trail by an A-frame. This way, the weight was shared between the limber and gun wheels and the barrel was supported, so that it did not vibrate unduly while on the move.

DATA

Calibre	155mm (6.10in)
Weight of gun and breech	9,595lb (4,352kg)
Total weight in action	30,600lb (13,880kg)
Barrel length	290in (7.366m)
Rifling	48 grooves, right-hand twist, one turn in 25 calibres
Recoil system and length	Hydro-pneumatic, variable 35 to 65in (889 to 165cm)
Breech mechanism	Asbury with Welin screw, percussion firing
Elevation	- 1 degrees 40' to + 63 degrees 20'
Traverse	30 degrees either side of zero
Shell weight	94.71lb (42.96kg)
Muzzle velocity	2,800ft/sec (853m/sec)
Maximum range	25,395 yards (23,221m)
Types of projectile available	HE; HE/AP; Chemical

British gunners in Italy prepare to fire a 155mm gun M1. The gun-layer for line, standing on the trail leg, is waiting for the gun-layer for elevation, on the other side of the gun, to finish elevating. Two loaders stand by with the next shell on the loading tray

The 8in Howitzer M1

distributed to armies all round the world. Many are still in use today. Some have newer and longer barrels to give more range, but many are exactly as they were made in 1941. In the US Army the M1 was re-designated M114 at some time in the 1960s, and is still in wide use.

The next First World War design to be overhauled was the 8in howitzer. The US Army had obtained a number of these from the British to equip their troops in France. Some had been manufactured in the USA, so the manufacturers were simply told to keep at it after they finished the British contract, and make more for American use. The Americans

Four men on ratchet spanners lowering the carriage and lifting the wheels off the ground to bring their 155mm gun into action

US gunners with a 155mm gun on a 'Kelly Mount', somewhere in the South Pacific in 1944. The carriage sits on a central pivot, and the trail ends ride on the circular rail so that the gun can be rapidly traversed to fire against ships (but not at this elevation, of course)

ended the war with three different marks of howitzer made in either country.

During the 1920s, the older designs were scrapped, but a few of the final mark (Mark 8½) were retained into the Second World War years as training weapons. Work on a new design began in 1919, resulting in a split-trail weapon with a range of 18,700 yards (17,155m) with a 200lb (91kg) shell, but the project was closed down in 1921 for the usual financial reason. It was revived in 1927,

The 155mm howitzer M1918 was a French First World War design, which, by 1939, had been given pneumatic tyres

The 155mm howitzer M1 was an entirely new design, with split trail and spring balancing gear

the intention being to provide a 'partner piece' for the 155mm gun – a howitzer barrel that would fit on the same mounting. Desultory work continued through the 1930s and the final design was standardized as the 8in Howitzer M1 in 1940.

Apart from the length of barrel, the result of this work looked just like the M1 gun, and even used the same breech mechanism. However, the inter-changeability of the two barrels was not as easy as it might have seemed; it was not simply a case of disconnecting the barrel from the recoil system, removing it and replacing it with the other barrel. The different weight, recoil force and balance meant that the entire top carriage had to be lifted off and the springs beneath the traversing ring changed; the pressure in the pneumatic equilibrators which

The 8in howitzer M1 shared the came carriage with the 155mm gun M1; the only obvious difference is the shorter barrel

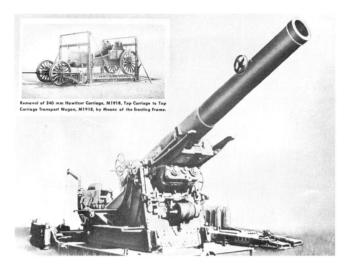

Removal of 240 mm Howitzer Carriage, M1918, Top Carriage to Top Carriage Transport Wagon, M1918, by Means of the Erecting Frame.

The 240mm howitzer M1918 has an elderly look about it; the wheel on the barrel, the 'prongs' sticking out alongside the recoil system, and the winch drum on the front are all part of the apparatus for putting the gun together by means of winches. The inset picture shows the mounting being lifted from its transport wagon

The 240mm M1918 on its modernized transport wagons

The first design of 240mm howitzer M1, showing how the gun was to be carried on a semi-trailer

The first model 240mm howitzer emplaced, showing the original carriage design with the semi-trailer connection at the front and the four-wheeled limber off to one side

balanced the muzzle weight had to be changed, and the nitrogen pressure inside the recuperator had to be adjusted. It was, in other words, a workshop job, and not one that could be done in half an hour with a hammer.

The M1 (and its modification, the M2, which differed only in the method of attaching the breech ring) was widely used during and after the war. It was taken out of US first-line service some time in the 1980s, but is still used by several other countries. It fired a 200lb (91kg) shell to a maximum range of 18,500 yards (16,970m).

The 240mm Howitzer

The last wartime design to require attention was the 240mm howitzer. The M1918 design had been purchased from Schneider in France and had a peculiar history. In the Russo-Japanese War, the Japanese put 28cm howitzers into the field to batter the defences of Port Arthur. The Russians decided that a similar weapon might be useful should they ever decide to wage war in Europe, since wherever they moved they would be faced with fortresses. They asked Schneider for a 28cm howitzer. The design was finally approved in 1911, several were delivered to Russia, and some were later built for the French Army in 1914–18.

When they entered the war, the Americans looked this 28cm weapon over in their search for a heavy howitzer, but preferred a calibre of 24cm. They asked Schneider to modify the Russian design accordingly. The design was drawn up, and arrangements were made to have the gun and mounting built in the USA. American officers and engineers were attached to Schneider to learn the techniques, and Schneider later sent engineers to the USA to help in setting up the production facilities. No less than 2,627 howitzers and 1,214 mountings were ordered, with production to commence early in 1918. The technical production problems were enormous, not least the manufacture of the hydro-pneumatic recoil system, and by the end of 1918 only one complete equipment had been built. The end of the war saw the contracts drastically curtailed, and in the end only 330 complete equipments were built. Even this was slow; the first equipment was sent to a proving round to be tested and blew up at the first shot, and it took a long time before production of a reliable howitzer was able to begin.

The M1918 was a ponderous weapon which, like most of its contemporaries, travelled in several pieces, and had to be laboriously assembled by means of hoists and ropes at the firing point. It fired a 345lb (156.8kg) shell to a range of 16,400 yards (15,045m),

240mm Howitzer M1 on Carriage M1

The US Army decided that a 240mm (9.45in) howitzer would be useful, bought a design from France in 1918, built 330 of them and lived to regret it. It was a poor design, and getting it to work properly ate up far too much of the slender budget in the 1920s. It was freely admitted that the only real solution would be to scrap the design and start again, but that was an unattainable dream. In 1934, there was a proposal to develop an improved carriage, more suitable for high-speed towing, but this came to nothing.

In 1939, the financial climate was improving and the drawings were brought out and studied, torn up, and a completely new equipment was designed. The howitzer itself was a straightforward enough design, using a screw breech with a dropping block balanced by springs, and more or less based upon the 16in gun breech. The mounting was to be a massive split-trail affair, which was to have the trail ends carried on a four-wheeled limber, and the front end curved up and forwards, so that it would hook on to a tractor in the same manner as a commercial articulated truck. The gun and its recoil system and cradle were to be carried as a separate load on a semi-trailer hooked to another tractor. However, it seems that the cross-country performance of this was not satisfactory, and the design was changed, doing away with the trailer connection and carrying the mounting on another six-wheeled trailer.

Towing was done by the Tractor, High-Speed, 38-ton M6 or, later, by various redundant tanks with their turrets removed. On arrival at the firing point, the mounting was slid from its trailer by winches on the tractors, the trails opened part-way, the barrel trailer winched up the trails, and the barrel unit winched off the trailer and on to the mounting. It was a long, hard job, also involving the digging of a massive pit between the trail legs to allow the breech to recoil at high elevations.

The design was standardized as the 240mm howitzer M1 in May 1943, and shortly afterwards a 20-ton motorized crane was attached to each gun battery. This towed a small trailer with a clamshell bucket, which was used to dig the pit. The crane lifted the mounting over the pit and positioned it, lifted the spades into the pit, then lifted the gun off its trailer and placed it on to the mounting. This reduced the emplacement time from about eight hours to about two, and was much less exhausting.

DATA

Calibre	240mm (9.45in)
Weight of gun and breech	25,261lb (11,458kg)
Total weight in action	64,700lb (29,348kg)
Barrel length	331 in (8.407m)
Rifling	68 grooves, right-hand twist, one turn in 25 calibres
Recoil system and length	Hydro-pneumatic, constant, 56in (142cm)
Breech mechanism	Interrupted screw, drop block, percussion firing
Elevation	+ 15 degrees to + 65 degrees
Traverse	22.5 degrees either side of zero
Shell weight	360lb (163.3kg)
Muzzle velocity	2,300ft/sec (701m/sec)
Maximum range	25,225 yards (23,065m)
Types of projectile available	HE only

240mm Howitzer M1 on Carriage M1 continued

The final, standardized, 240mm howitzer M1. No spades are fitted here, as it is on a concrete gunpark. The curved rail between the trail legs is to rest the rear end of a loading tray on, the front end resting in the breech

but it was not considered to be as accurate as had been hoped, and its range was disappointing. In 1924–25, a long and exhaustive series of trials led to the conclusion that the only proper remedy would be to scrap the equipment and design something better; with 330 brand-new howitzers in stock, however, this was hardly practical.

In 1934, an 'interim solution' was proposed – the design of an improved carriage, better suited to high-speed towing. However, although this would improve manoeuvre, it would do nothing for the ballistic shortcomings, and that idea was quietly dropped. It was brought out again in 1939 and, after a great deal of discussion, in April 1940, the decision to design a completely fresh weapon was taken.

The 240mm Howitzer M1 was standardized in May 1943, and was a first-class weapon. It saw a great deal of use in the Italian campaign in 1943–45, and it was to remain in use in the British and US Armies until the late 1950s, when the wartime stock of ammunition was finally expended.

The howitzer fired a 360lb (163.6kg) shell to a range of 25,225 yards (23,140m) with commendable accuracy. In late 1944, there was an interesting proposal to fit the carriage with tracked suspension and pull the barrel back, disconnected from the recoil system, so as to distribute the weight. This would allow the howitzer to be moved in one piece, by a suitably powerful tractor, for short tactical displacements. This idea was followed by a suggestion for a 240mm gun as a

The 240mm mounting on its transport wagon

The 38-ton High Speed Tractor M6, used for towing the 240mm howitzer and 8in gun

Loading the 240mm howitzer; the bag charge is being pushed up the loading tray and into the chamber

'partner piece', with a range of 45,000 yards (41,280m). This gun would be 70 calibres long (just over 55ft, or about 17m), and it was felt that it might be easier to design the carriage so that it could be slung between two tractors, one at each end, making the gun more manoeuvrable. The war ended and the project was dropped, but it is interesting to note that the 280mm M65 'Atomic Cannon' of the 1950s adopted the very same idea.

The 8in Gun M1

Only one American heavy equipment did not have a First World War ancestor. The 8in gun M1 was developed in response to the demand in the Westervelt Report for a heavy gun of about 8in,

The 240mm Howitzer M1 made its last appearance in Korea. Here is the gun of the 213th FA battalion, 45th Infantry Division, north of Yang-gu in 1953

(a) The 8in gun M1 barrel arriving on its transport wagon; the 20-ton Lorain crane in the background would have lifted it off

(b) Another location, but the next stage in the assembly of the 8in gun, as the barrel is carefully lowered into place. Four lugs on the cradle have to mate with four bolts on the carriage, requiring a deft touch by the crane operator and the men on the guiding rope

(c) The assembly continues, with everybody holding their breath. The four bolts were about 3in in diameter, and nuts were run down and tightened once the barrel unit was in place. That was all that transferred the recoil shock from the cradle to the mounting

(d) The final result: the 8in gun M1 in position. The tank beneath the barrel was the nitrogen pressure tank for the barrel-balancing apparatus; the roller above it was part of the machinery for assembling the gun to the carriage by means of winches, when no crane was available

firing to about 35,000 yards (32,110m).

Some work had been done on the idea in 1920, largely aimed at adapting the coast-defence 8in gun, currently being used on a railway mounting, to a road-mobile weapon. However, this 32-calibre gun, with a maximum range of about 24,000 yards (22,020m), came nowhere near the Westervelt demand, so the project was dropped in 1924.

In 1939, the suggestion was made to develop a really powerful new 8in gun as a partner piece for the 240mm howitzer, to fit on the same mounting. Work on this began in June 1940, and resulted in the 8in Gun T2. Its maximum range of 33,500 yards (30,735m) fell slightly short of the original demand, but was deemed close enough. The new gun was 50 calibres long, and had a muzzle velocity of some 2,800 feet per second, and this led to problems with excessive bore wear and a lack of accuracy.

Various modifications were tried: the T2E1 used the British Probert rifling system, with a shell having a forward centring band as well as a normal driving band; the T2E2 had a different rifling twist; the T2E3 had a chromium-plated bore; the T2E4 had Probert rifling chromium-plated; the T2E5 used pre-engraved projectiles. None of them showed any superiority over the original T2 design and eventually, in January 1944, this was standardized as the M1. It was appreciated that it was not entirely satisfactory but, since nothing better seemed likely to appear, the T2 was accepted. Comparatively few were made, since practical use also revealed that the long gun barrel was unstable on its transport trailer over

rough country. Even so, it was put to good use; the US 1st Army in Europe had nine guns, which between them fired 18,935 rounds between D-Day and VE Day.

RUSSIA

The 203mm Howitzer Model 1931

The heavy artillery in use by the Soviet Army in 1939–45 is really limited to the 152mm group of weapons. Very little is known about Second World War Russian heavier artillery, and the only equipment of this kind seen in wartime pictures is the 203mm Howitzer Model 1931.

In spite of its title, the Howitzer Model 1931 was not introduced into service until 1934, and it subsequently went through about six minor modifications before the final design was settled, probably in 1938–39. It was a perfectly conventional 8in howitzer, mounted on a box-trail carriage allowing 4 degrees of traverse on either side of zero, and 60 degrees of elevation; this allowed it to fire a 220lb (100kg) shell to a maximum range of 19,700 yards (18,075m). Once the design had been perfected, three variations appeared. The first production had two large wheels on the carriage, with a small-wheeled limber supporting the trail ends. The next type, few of which seem to have been produced, had small wheels on both carriage and limber; and the final and most common model used a tracked suspension unit on the carriage and a large-wheeled limber. The

The Soviet 203mm howitzer on its unique tracked carriage

Rear view of the Soviet 203mm howitzer, displayed at Aberdeen Proving Ground, USA

tracked suspension system closely resembled the standard Soviet tracked agricultural tractor of the period in its design; one supposes that the same production line was responsible for both.

Other Models

Some reports mention a 21cm Gun Model 39/40, but it seems that this was actually a German weapon, the 21cm K39/40 which had been captured on the Eastern Front in small numbers. It fired a 300lb (136kg) shell to a range of 33,270 yards (30,520m). Similarly, the 28cm Howitzer M1939 and the 30.5cm Howitzer M39/40 were probably Polish or Czech weapons, either taken in Poland in 1939 or captured from the Germans on the Eastern Front. None saw much employment.

Generally, it seems that the Soviet Army was content with its 152mm armoury, which produced all the firepower it required and was mobile enough to keep up with the action. Heavier weapons might have their uses, but their slowness in deployment was a drawback, and their production time meant fewer weapons reaching the troops; in the time taken to make these heavy weapons, a larger number of 152mm guns could be turned out. Also, in the 'Stormovik' ground-attack aircraft, the Russians had the replacement for heavy artillery that had been promised to other armies, but which rarely appeared.

The 152 mm Model 1910 Gun

The 152mm group – consisting of guns and howitzers – represented the major component of the supporting artillery strength in all their operations. The calibre (6in) dates back to the 1870s in Russian service, and had featured in the major re-equipment programme which took place prior to 1914. When, in the 1930s, the time came to look at this group of weapons, the first move was familiar: find the best surviving 152mm weapon, and bring it up to date as an interim measure. The result was the Model 1910/30 gun.

The Model 1910 gun had been designed by Schneider of France; it was advanced for its day,

with many features that were to become Schneider trademarks, such as the screw breech, a shell-retaining clip in the chamber, and advanced sights. It was moved in two parts, the barrel on a four-wheeled wagon and the carriage on its own two wheels and a limber. This made two horse loads, but in later years, when tractors became available, it was common to pull both loads behind one tractor. This was now taken and modified; the carriage was given smaller wheels, the elevation reduced to a maximum of 37 degrees instead of 40, and the ammunition improved to increase the range from 12,400m (13,515 yards) to 17,100m (18,640 yards). It remained, though, a two-part load and, after considering the matter, the designers went back and tried again. This time, they scrapped the original carriage and produced a split-trail pattern; the gun was mounted further forward and given twin spring equilibrators to balance the muzzle weight, and the gun could be pulled back for transport in one piece. This became the M1910/34; the elevation now increased to 45 degrees, there were 29 degrees of traverse each side of zero, and the charge was reduced in order to reduce the recoil force, so that the maximum range dropped slightly to 16,200m (17,660 yards). This seemed to be a sound design, and production began in 1934, replacing the M1910/30.

The 152mm Gun M1935

The army was of the opinion, however, that more range could be achieved in this calibre, and in the following year a completely new design appeared. This seems to have been developed in concert with the 203mm howitzer, since it used the same box-trail carriage with tracked suspension. This restricted the amount of traverse, cutting it down to 4 degrees each side, but the elevation went up to 60 degrees. The gun was 50 calibres long and could fire a 45kg shell at 880m/sec to reach a maximum range of 27,000m (29,400 yards). This went into service as the 152mm Gun M1935. This was very good performance but at a price: the equipment weighed 19 tons behind the tractor, and 18 tons in the firing position, which was about 10 tons heavier than the M1910/34 equipment. As a result, it was only built in relatively small numbers, and the designers had to go back to try again.

The 152mm Gun-Howitzer Model 1934

Meanwhile, another 152mm gun had appeared from another design bureau; this design was intended as a partner piece for the same carriage as used with the 122mm gun M31. This took the barrel of the M1910 and added a 'pepperpot' muzzle brake to reduce the recoil to a level the lighter carriage could stand. The carriage was a two-wheeled split-trail pattern, with spring equilibrator horns in front of the shield – now something of a Russian trademark – and the trail ends supported on a two-wheeled limber for towing. It fired a 43.5kg shell to 17,600m (19,185 yards), and entered service as the 152mm Gun-Howitzer Model 1934; it was called a gun-howitzer because it was provided with several charge zones, the topmost of which gave it a velocity of 655m/sec, allowing it to produce a gun-like trajectory, while the smaller charges gave it a howitzer capability.

The 152mm Gun-Howitzer M1937

This was reasonably well received, but the army thought it could be improved by being given more

elevation. This duly appeared as the 152mm Gun-Howitzer M1937, which got its title from being 30 calibres long, and having a maximum elevation of 65 degrees and twelve charge zones. At top charge it performed as a gun, with a maximum range of 17,265m (18,820 yards) with a 43.5kg shell; it also had an armour-piercing shell, which could go through 125mm of armour at 1,000m (1,090 yards) range.

This performance was rather a surprise for 1937, and the twelve charges gave it a bewildering choice of trajectories, allowing it to drop shells behind cover at virtually any range. Although the maximum range was about a kilometre less than that of the M1935 gun, its versatility and its weight – only 7 tons – more than compensated for that, and it became the principal heavy weapon of the Soviet Army. In post-war years it was generously handed out to the Warsaw Pact and other countries, and many are still in existence.

The 152mm Howitzer M1938

In the following year, the 152mm Howitzer M1938 appeared. This was a lighter and handier weapon than the gun-howitzers, but it threw a 51kg shell to 12,400 yards (11,375m), and was no more than 4.1 tons in weight. It was also a great deal easier and cheaper to produce than the larger 152mm weapons; the carriage was that of the 122mm M1938 howitzer, a split-trail with shield and

Loading the Soviet 152mm gun-howitzer M1937

The Soviet 152mm gun/howitzer M1937 in travelling mode, with the barrel disconnected from the recoil system and pulled back so as to distribute the weight between the wheels

The Soviet 152mm howitzer M1938, essentially an enlarged 122mm design

rubber-tyred wheels, and the barrel was carried on the usual type of trough cradle.

The 152mm Howitzer M1943

With this varied armoury in production, the Russians entered the war and, rather than interfere with production by ordering new designs, they wisely stayed with what they knew, and produced them by the thousand. However, the stresses and strains of war soon told on the M1938 howitzer; putting a 152mm barrel on the lighter carriage had over-stressed it, and by 1942 there was an urgent need to replace it with a better and stronger design.

The carriage was re-designed in a stronger form; the howitzer was given a large double-baffle muzzle brake, and the recoil system was changed, so that the barrel now moved in a ring cradle, with the recuperator and buffer cylinders above and below the barrel. The weight came down to 3.5 tons, but the equipment was far more reliable, and it went into service as the 152mm howitzer M1943. Its reliability has been well proven; it served throughout the war, is still in Russian reserves and training establishments, and is in first-line service with a dozen or more armies around the world, from Chile to Mongolia.

4   Anti-Aircraft Artillery

DEFENCE AGAINST THE BOMBER

In the 1930s, the prospect of war meant only one thing for most people; the prospect of fleets of aircraft raining down bombs, and particularly gas bombs. As a result, the defence against aircraft had a high priority when it came to political rhetoric, although rather less of a priority when it came to distributing money and actually constructing some form of defence. When Prime Minister Stanley Baldwin stood up in the House of Commons in November 1932 and said, 'I think it is well for the man in the street to realize that there is no power on earth that can prevent him from being bombed. Whatever people may tell him, the bomber will always get through. . .', he was simply telling the truth as it stood at that moment.

Detection

The only defence against bombers was exactly what it had been in 1918: a combination of guns on the ground, and standing patrols of aircraft in the sky covering the likely approach routes. At the time, the number of guns defending Britain was probably less than a hundred, many lacking spare parts, while the fighter strength of the RAF was insufficient to permit standing patrols to be flown for more than a few days. The only method of detecting aircraft was either by eye, relying upon the Observer Corps and other alerting organizations, or by sound, relying upon huge concrete 'sound mirrors' erected in likely places (Romney Marshes, the Thames Estuary, the Yorkshire moors). These were supposed to collect the sound of approaching aircraft engines, reflect it into a microphone and deliver it to an operator.

Other decisions were being taken, and factories began to receive orders for aircraft and guns. The orders were based upon a gradual increase in strength, which would put 136 guns and 1,008 searchlights in place by March 1940, and 464 guns and 2,400 lights by 1946. Fighter aircraft strength would increase to twenty-five squadrons over the same period. Most significantly, the orientation of the defences shifted from a possible French threat to a probable German threat. This meant that most of the sound mirrors were in the wrong places and were redundant. They could be forgotten, but for the fact that to scrap them would have pointed towards the fact that something else was in use. They were left in place, therefore, and one or two new ones were actually built facing Germany, to keep up the pretence.

Radar

At about the same time, a miracle happened: RDF, or Radio Direction Finding, was invented, later called 'Radar'. The RDF name was used as a cover; radio direction finding had been in use since the earliest days of radio, so anybody who heard about RDF assumed it was just a new and improved method of applying the old principles. Most people did not hear much about it at all.

Similar ideas had occurred to scientists in other countries. Late in 1935, the Germans had carried out experiments, and in 1936 issued a contract for their first early-warning radar set. The US Army and US Navy had also, by this time, developed experimental radar sets, while the French were working on a maritime radar for providing early warning of icebergs. This work was soon directed towards air defence. The significant difference was that the British developed a coherent defensive system of radars, observers, communications and control rooms, which ensured that the information which was extracted was sent to the place where it would do the most good. Other countries merely had radar sets.

The Power of the Bomber

Events in Abyssinia, and the Spanish Civil War, pointed to the possible power of the bomber. Unfortunately, most of the 'eye-witness' reports were exaggerated, particularly from Spain, where reports were issued via the appropriate political propaganda machine, so that what finally appeared in the newspapers was calculated to frighten rather than to inform. However, it did concentrate the mind on the threat, and provided the stimulus, without which the development of radar and other defensive measures might have been smothered by committees.

THE BOMBER TARGETS

By 1936, it was apparent that defence against aircraft was becoming more complex. It seemed that modern designs of aircraft appeared every week, and every one flew faster or higher than the one before. Moreover, the aircraft had very different characteristics – there was the high-flying bomber, the dive-bomber, the low-flying ground-attack machine, the fighter, the transport – no one gun could hope to compete against every type of target.

The gun to fight the high-flying bomber needed to be very powerful, in order to throw the shell up to high altitude in the shortest possible time. On the other hand, the gun to fight the dive-bomber or ground-attack aircraft, moving low and fast, needed to be much more manoeuvrable – able to swing quickly, to track a fast-moving target. It also needed

a high rate of fire, to get as many rounds off as possible in the short time during which the target was within range. Hitherto, the bomber had been the only target considered, and the existing guns had been developed with it in mind. Now, it seemed, lighter guns were going to be needed to deal with the low-flyers.

OERLIKON AND BOFORS

These requirements opened the door for two enterprising armaments firms in neutral countries to make their names known across the world. The Oerlikon Machine Tool Company of Zurich had, in the 1920s, acquired the patents for a 20mm automatic gun, designed by a German engineer named Becker during the First World War. They then perfected the design and promoted it as a light anti-aircraft cannon, selling it to several countries. The Oerlikon gun was simply an overgrown machine gun, firing small shells filled with high explosive, or solid piercing shot, at abut 500–600 rounds per minute, and it was to prove a useful deterrent against the low-flyer.

The second contender in the light-gun field was the Swedish company Bofors AB. They had been in the armaments business for many years, providing field- and coast-defence artillery to several countries, but without achieving much fame. In 1929, they developed a light anti-aircraft gun of 40mm (2.244in) calibre, which fired at the astonishing rate of 120 rounds per minute. It soon found a market and was eventually adopted by virtually all the combatants during the Second World War.

FIRE CONTROL

A Three-Dimensional Problem

The most difficult problem in the 1930s was fire control. In the 1920s, work had begun on improving the 'central post' instruments of the First World War, so as to provide a rapid answer to 'the anti-aircraft problem'. The problem was simply how to

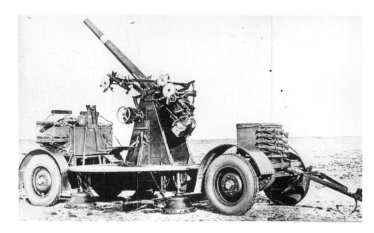

The British 3in 20-cwt gun, which stayed in service with the field armies for some time after the arrival of the 3.7in guns

put the shell and the aircraft in the same place at the same time. The gunner was confronted with a target moving at high speed and capable of moving in any direction except backwards. The shell took a certain time to reach the aircraft's altitude. The question was, where would the aircraft be when the shell got up there?

The answer to this question was based on one fundamental assumption: during the shell's flight, the aircraft would continue on the same course and at the same speed. This was not as unlikely as it might sound – the bomber could not hope to drop his bombs with any accuracy if he was jinking all over the sky, nor could he afford to waste fuel by performing aerobatics over enemy country.

Based on this assumption, the problem became a simple matter of three-dimensional geometry, provided some figures were known, including the speed of the aircraft, the velocity of the shell, the wind speed and its direction, and so on. All these

could be measured, but what was needed was a mechanical calculator, which would produce a faster answer than could be achieved with trigonometrical tables, slide-rule, pencil and paper.

Predictors

The 'central post instrument' of the First World War was a simple geared telescope device, which allowed the observer to track the aircraft by turning hand-wheels. These were coupled to electrical generators, so that the speed of tracking was reflected in a voltage; a meter could be calibrated to work out the target speed and height. Instrument makers, such as the Sperry Gyroscope company, now built on this idea, and developed instruments which could be set with the wind speed, shell velocity and other factors. Then, by tracking the aircraft, it was possible to calculate where the aircraft would be at the end of the shell's flight, and

One of the first 3.7in guns to leave the factory in 1936. The complexity and expense of the design is apparent. For some reason, the outriggers have not been fitted

thus deduce a 'future position', to which the gun would be directed.

These instruments, known as 'predictors' in British service and 'directors' in American service, began as entirely mechanical devices. Gradually, they adopted more electrical features until, driven by the electronic revolution begun by radar, during the course of the war, they became entirely electronic. (However, they did not in any way operate like a modern computer. In today's parlance, these were 'analogue' devices, using or generating electrical currents and voltages that were proportional to the information they represented.)

The next stage of development was to apply the output of the predictor directly to the gun by wire, so that the elevation, azimuth and fuze setting could be displayed on dials, and acted upon. This was relatively simple, and was in use before 1930. The next step was to make life a little easier for the gun-layer by adopting the 'follow-the-pointer' dial. This was a dial with two pointers, one actuated by the predictor, the other actuated by operating the controls of the gun. To direct the weapon in azimuth, for instance, the gun-layer had to watch the azimuth dial, and keep his pointer constantly over the predictor pointer by adjusting the traversing hand-wheel on the gun mounting. This system was in universal use by the late 1930s.

Remote Power Operation

The ultimate goal was to fit the gun mounting with electric motors controlled by the signals from the predictor. As the predictor tracked the aircraft, the gun would be tracking the future position without the gun-layer having to touch anything. All the gun's detachment had to do was throw ammunition into the breech as fast as they could and pull the firing lever. This 'Remote Power Operation' took much longer to achieve; actually driving a gun by remote control was not very difficult, but driving it and achieving the precise position demanded for accurate gunfire was far more complicated. The US Army had a power-operated 105mm gun working in

1930, but it took another twelve years before it was working accurately enough to put the shell where the predictor wanted it, and was reliable enough to meet the demands of field service.

AMMUNITION

The First World War saw a wide range of likely projectiles tried as anti-aircraft shells; high explosive, shrapnel, and incendiary all had their day. The problem of developing a time fuze accurate enough to burst the shell reliably in the right area had taken most of the First World War to solve. Now, the guns were getting bigger and the ranges and altitudes greater, so the designs had to be re-worked. The optimum combination, it was realized, would be a high-explosive shell fitted with an accurate clockwork time fuze. Design and production facilities for mass production of mechanical fuzes had to be assembled and put to work and that, of course, meant money.

Eventually everything fell into place, and by 1939 most countries had the equipment they required, in quality if not in quantity. Once the war had begun, production and development were both stepped up and, because the performance of aircraft improved, the guns had to improve in order to remain effective.

BRITAIN

Between the Wars

At the end of the First World War, the standard British AA gun was the 3in 20-cwt, mounted either on a four-wheeled trailer platform or on a motor lorry. There was also a large number of other guns, which had been developed during the war but which were almost immediately made obsolete, leaving the 3in as the sole air-defence weapon. Under development was a 3.6in gun of considerable promise, but with the end of the war this work was stopped, and the design abandoned, even though it had been approved for service. The AA artillery branch was gradually

The 3.7in gun on the static Mounting Mark 2C with remote power control and fuze setting and ramming machine

The 3.7in gun in the firing position; the wheels would normally be removed

run down until only a single brigade was left, and there it remained for several years.

Behind the scenes, however, some technical progress was made. A mechanical time fuze was designed (copied from a captured German specimen), and a few were made for trials; designs of AA guns were discussed, a predictor was developed, data transmission from predictor to gun was perfected, height-finders, sound locators and other instruments were produced and tested.

By 1928, opinions on a new AA gun had settled on 'a 3.7in gun firing a 25lb (11.35kg) shell with a ceiling of, say, 28,000ft'. Six years elapsed before finance was approved, then, in 1934, a specification was given to Woolwich Arsenal and to Vickers-Armstrong, requesting designs. The Vickers was selected, and their first pilot model passed its acceptance tests in April 1936. Production began in April 1937, the first guns being issued to a service unit in January 1938. Thereafter, production increased and continued until 1945, averaging a delivery rate of 228 guns per month over that period.

Ceilings

In its original form, the 3.7in Mark 1 gun fired a 28lb (12.75kg) high-explosive shell fitted with the 'Fuze, Time, No. 199', a powder-burning fuze, to an effective ceiling of 23,500ft. A short explanation of the meaning of the word 'ceiling' might be appropriate here.

Any AA gun can have three different 'ceilings', and it is not always clear which is being quoted in performance figures. In most cases, it is the 'maximum ceiling', the height which the projectile will reach if the gun is at its maximum elevation and the time fuze is not operating. If the maximum is 25,000ft, this describes an arc in the sky 25,000ft from the gun's trunnions. As soon as the elevation moves from the maximum, the ceiling drops, as the line of fire swings round this imaginary arc. In the late 1920s, the maximum time of flight of the shell was governed by the time fuze; once it reached its maximum time, it detonated the shell. This point was inevitably lower than the maximum ceiling, and was known as the 'operational ceiling'. Again, this describes an arc in the sky at the gun's maximum elevation, an arc representing the end of

A 3.7in gun on the Mark 2 travelling carriage; there are small differences in the outriggers, jacks and other simplifications for ease of production

A closer view of the breech area of the 3.7 on Mark 2C mounting, showing the fuze-setter/rammer with its loading tray folded over, and also the heavy counterweight, which stretched above and behind the breech. The square box (top centre) is the fuze-setting machine, and the semi-circular plate on it is the switch that set the fuze-setter and rammer in action

the fuze time. As soon as the elevation of the gun is changed, the operational ceiling drops.

More important is the 'effective ceiling', which is generally defined as the height at which the gun will be able to fire a series of shells at a moving target. The precise definition varied from time to time as targets got faster or flew higher; in the late 1930s, the definition was 'that height at which a directly approaching target at 400mph can be engaged for 20 seconds before the gun reaches 70 degrees elevation'. The maximum ceiling of the 3.7in gun was 41,000ft (12,500m), but, based on this rule, the effective ceiling was only 23,500ft (7,165m). The best that could be said was that it left plenty of room for expansion, and this arrived fairly quickly in the shape of a mechanical time fuze which added another 1,100ft to the effective ceiling.

The 3.7in gun could also be used as a ground support gun, with a maximum range of 15,800 yards. This is a Mark 2 mounting, firing in Italy in 1943

A 3.7in gun of the London defences in action in November 1940

The Predictor

The predictor was another limiting factor. Obviously, in the design of predictors there had to be a set of limiting figures, defining the maximum altitude and speed of the proposed target. If the target chose to fly higher or faster, the predictor was unable to produce a sensible answer. Once the enemy had aircraft exceeding the values designed into the predictor, either the predictor had to be modified (by changing the various cams and gears in the largely mechanical devices), or it had to be replaced by a better model with higher design performance.

In the case of the 3.7in gun, this progression can be charted. With the Predictor No. 1 and Fuze 199 there was an effective ceiling of 23,500ft; with the

Fuze 208 (mechanical), this went up to 24,600, which was as much as the predictor could handle. The arrival of Predictor No. 2 raised the Fuze 208 figure to 25,300ft; there was then a modification of the predictor, which lifted it to 29,400ft; finally, the largely electronic predictor No. 11 brought the figure to 32,000ft. Throughout all these changes, the ceiling for the Fuze 199 remained at 23,500, since in that case the fuze-burning time of 30 seconds was the limiting factor. The Fuze 208, on the other hand, had a running time of 43 seconds, which allowed ample room for the predictors to catch up.

MFS

The gun was also improved. In its original form, the fuzes were set by hand, using a 'fuze key' – rather like a large ring spanner – to turn the time ring to the desired setting. This process took time and care. The complete round, which weighed 50lb (22.6kg), was then hand-loaded into the breech, and the gun was fired manually. This limited the rate of fire to eight rounds per minute. In 1939 came the first 'Machine, Fuze Setting' (MFS), a box with a follow-the-pointer dial; the gunner set the machine pointer to match the predictor pointer, and another gunner then entered the nose of the shell into a hole in the box; then, a mechanical key gripped the fuze and set the time ring. The gunner then withdrew the round and loaded it.

Improved models of MFS followed, until finally the MFS No. 11 appeared, in 1942; this was attached to the gun cradle and consisted of a tray into which the loading gunner dropped the round. He hit a switch and the tray lifted and dropped the round into the loading tray; the round was thrust forward, so that the fuze entered the setter, was set, and then withdrew, and the loading tray swung across to position the round behind the breech. A rammer drove the round into the gun, the breech closed, the loading tray returned to the setting position, and the gun fired automatically. Meanwhile, the loader had dropped another round on the tray and hit the switch, so that as soon as the loading tray came back, the next round was dropped in and the fuze setting began. This increased the rate of fire to nineteen rounds per minute.

This system offered a further benefit. With hand fuze-setting and loading, the time lag between setting the fuze and firing the gun – known as the 'dead time' – was variable, depending upon the state of training of the gunners, and their physical condition. The speed they could achieve with the first rounds of an engagement was higher than that achieved three or four hours later during a long night of constant alerts and air raids. The MFS 11, however, gave a constant 'dead time' of 3.05 seconds for the first round, and 2.5 seconds for every subsequent round. The importance of this lay in the business of prediction. When the fuze length was predicted, it had to include an allowance for the time taken between setting and firing, since the predicted fuze length was timed from firing to target. If the actual time varied, the prediction was in error by the difference between the assumed 'dead time' and the real time. With a fixed 'dead time', prediction became much more accurate, and there was a significant improvement in the ratio of shells fired to hits obtained.

Improving the 3.7in Gun

By 1941, the performance of aircraft was overtaking the performance of the gun, and in January of that year the War Office demanded a new design of gun capable of reaching up to 50,000ft in 30 seconds, with the ability to fire three rounds and have the fourth in the chamber in 20 seconds. Four possible solutions were offered: an existing Naval 5.25in gun; the 5.25in gun with the bore reduced to 4.5in, but with the chamber taking the 5.25in cartridge; the 5.25 reduced to 3.7in calibre; or the existing 4.5in AA gun reduced in bore to 3.7in, and using the existing 4.5in cartridge. After some debate, the 5.25in gun was chosen as the long-term solution. However, these were large and complex guns, and the Royal Navy had first call on them, so provision in sufficient numbers would be slow. As an 'interim solution', the 4.5in gun, linered down to 3.7in bore, would be adopted until enough 5.25in guns were available.

An experimental gun was built and became the Mark 5. However, it was soon obvious that a 4.5in cartridge behind a 3.7in shell pushed it out at such a velocity that the erosive wear was staggering, and the accuracy life very short. Such a gun in service would need a new barrel after every air raid.

The 3.7in Mark 6

At this crucial time, Colonel Probert of the Armaments Research Department had just perfected a system of rifling that promised to solve the wear problem. The gun was rifled with grooves, which gradually became more shallow as they went up the gun bore until they disappeared altogether about three calibres back from the muzzle.

Ordnance, QF, 3.7in Guns

This, the British standard medium AA gun from 1936 to the mid-1960s, was first proposed in 1928. Specifications were drawn up, and in 1934 orders were given to Woolwich Arsenal and to Vickers to produce a solution. The Vickers design was accepted and went into production in 1937, the first guns reaching units in January 1938.

It was an extremely advanced design for its time; unlike every other AA gun, it had rudimentary sights intended solely for emergency use, receiving all its information electrically from the predictor and displaying it on dials. All the gun-layers had to do was to operate the gun controls so that the dial pointers were continuously matched, while the rest of the detachment loaded and fired. The original carriage was highly complex and, at 8 tons, well over the specified weight, upsetting those who were used to the lighter and handier 3in gun. However, its performance put it ahead of any competition and it soon converted the doubters.

The gun was constantly improved during the war. Perhaps the greatest single improvement was the Molins fuse-setter/rammer, an electrically operated unit that doubled the rate of fire. The mountings, both mobile and static, were simplified in the interest of faster and easier production. Remote power control came into use in 1944, and the combination of this, with the latest radars and predictors and the proximity fuze, gave the guns an 82 per cent success rate against the V-1 flying bombs in 1944–45. The average number of shots fired for one V-1 was about 150, a vast improvement on the 18,500 shots per aircraft downed in the night blitz of 1940, when radar was in the teething stage and powder-filled time fuzes still standard.

Even so, the Army looked ahead and as early as January 1941 set forth specifications for an improved gun. As described elsewhere, this resulted in what was, in effect, a 4.5-in gun with a 3.7-in barrel, known as the 3.7 Mark 6 gun. It was only ever used on static mountings, since these took just over half the time to build as did mobile mountings, and in any case the 4.5in gun was too big for a mobile mounting. In post-war years it formed the basis of the last AA gun approved for British service, called 'Longhand', which was virtually a belt-fed 3.7in Mark 6 gun capable of firing at almost 80 rounds per minute.

A 3.7in Mark 6 gun. Note that the platform is bolted down into the emplacement and has no outriggers; there was no mobile version of this gun

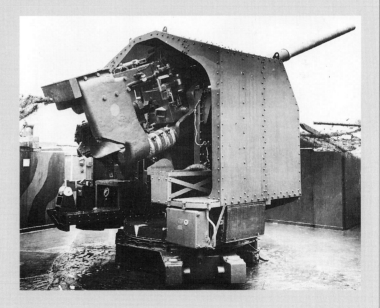

Ordnance, QF, 3.7in Guns continued

DATA (Mark 3 gun on Mark 2 carriage)

Calibre	3.7in (95mm)
Weight of gun and breech	3,931lb (1,783kg)
Total weight in action	20,541lb (9,317kg) (mobile mounting)
Barrel length	195.15in (4.956m)
Rifling	28 grooves, right-hand twist, one turn in 30 calibres
Recoil system and length	Hydro-pneumatic, constant, 32in (81mm)
Breech mechanism	Horizontal sliding block, semi-automatic, percussion firing
Elevation	- 5 degrees to + 80 degrees
Traverse	360 degrees
Shell weight	28lb (12.7kg)
Muzzle velocity	2,600ft/sec (792m/sec)
Effective ceiling	32,000ft (9,754m)
Types of projectile available:	HE; Shrapnel; AP.

DATA (Mark 6 Gun on Mark 2 Mounting)

Calibre	3.7in (95mm)
Weight of gun and breech	38,360lb (17,400kg)
Barrel length	252in (6.40m)
Rifling	28 grooves, right-hand, one turn in 27 calibres
Recoil system and length	Hydro-pneumatic, constant, 18in (457mm)
Breech mechanism	Horizontal sliding block, semi-automatic, percussion firing
Elevation	0 degrees to + 80 degrees
Traverse	360 degrees
Shell weight	28lb (12.7 kg)
Muzzle velocity	3,470ft/sec (1,058m/sec)
Effective ceiling	45,000ft (13,716m)

The special shell to go with this rifling had a high-efficiency driving band in the usual place, but it also had a 'centring band' at the shoulder. These bands were designed to be squeezed down by the shallowing grooves and smooth-bore muzzle, so that the shell emerged with the bands smoothed down and no surfaces were presented to cause air drag. (Only the driving bands were squeezed down; there was no resemblance between this and the taper-bore guns used by Germany.) A barrel rifled in this manner was tried and found successful, and went into production as the 3.7in Mark 6 gun, together with its special ammunition.

The Mark 6 went into production in 1943 and, far from being an 'interim' weapon, it stayed in service until the AA gun was superseded by the Air Defence Missile in 1959. It fired the special 28lb (12.75kg) HE shell at 3,425ft/sec (1,044m/sec) to a maximum ceiling of 59,300ft (18,075m), and an effective ceiling of 45,000ft (13,715m), far out-performing any other AA gun of comparable calibre.

The 5.25in Mark 1A and Mark 1B

The 5.25in gun that had been proposed as the long-term solution was an existing Naval dual-purpose equipment, capable of AA or surface fire. It promised the desired ballistic performance, and the Army received three twin mountings from the Navy

Right side of a 4.5in gun on travelling platform,

Left side of the 4.5in gun on travelling platform

in 1942, and began trials. As a result, it was decided to design two single-gun mountings.

The first of these was the Mark 1A, intended purely as an AA weapon. The gun was mounted in an open-backed mild steel shield in a circular concrete emplacement. An underground engine room contained a diesel generator and hydraulic pump, which provided the electrical and hydraulic

Loading the 4.5in gun, London, 1941

power for traverse, elevation, fuze setting, ramming and various other tasks.

The Mark 1B mounting was generally similar, but had the gun installed in an armoured turret. It was designed for use as a dual-purpose anti-aircraft/coast-defence (AA/CD) weapon.

The 4.5in Gun Mark 2

In the pre-war period, the variety of possible targets had led to the categorizing of guns as either light, medium or heavy. The medium group was filled by the existing 3in 20-cwt and the new 3.7in guns. The heavy group had a lesser priority, but by 1937 it was time to select a suitable weapon.

For several years, a 4.7in gun had been proposed as being of a suitable calibre for permanent mounting in defence of naval bases and similar vulnerable points. In view of the expense and effort required to get the 3.7in gun into production, it was suggested that the army might consider adopting an existing naval 4.5in weapon. The ballistics were

The 4.5in could be sited on the coast as a dual-purpose AA and coast weapon, as seen here

close to the proposed 4.7in design, the ammunition was in production, and, since most of the heavy guns would be close to naval bases and dockyards, the supply of ammunition by the Admiralty supply organization would be simple. As a result, the 4.5in gun Mark 2 entered military service in 1938.

The gun was mounted on a static pedestal that could be bolted down into a concrete emplacement; for movement, it was provided with a special transporting limber, which simply attached four wheels to the pedestal base, and allowed the complete equipment to be towed from place to place. Operation was entirely manual, although an electric rammer was fitted in 1940, which allowed a rate of fire of eight rounds per minute to be reached. The shell weighed 54lb (24.5kg), and with a muzzle velocity of 2,400ft/sec, it could reach a maximum ceiling of 44,000ft. Guns mounted in suitable positions close to the sea could also be used as anti-ship weapons, having a maximum horizontal range of 22,800 yards (20,920m); these were generally on the Mounting Mark 1A, which allowed 9.5 degrees of depression to allow close-in firing at sea level. The guns were supplied with armour-piercing shells for the coast-defence role.

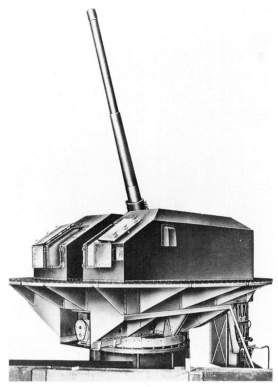

The 5.25in gun on single mounting, before installation into its emplacement

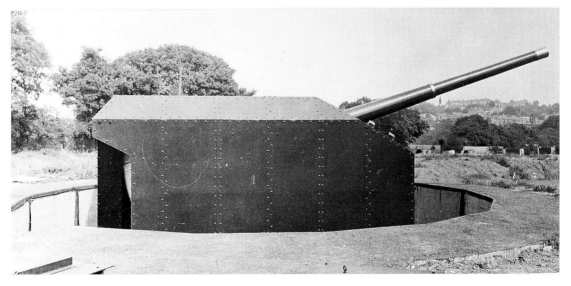

The 5.25in emplaced and ready for action

The complicated internals concealed by the 5.25in gun's turret

Light Weapons

Having dealt with the heavy and medium side of the defences, the authorities turned to the light weapons for defence against ground-attack aircraft and other low-flyers. Several countries had adopted the 20mm Oerlikon gun, but the British, feeling that the shell was too light to be effective, looked for something heavier. In 1936, another short-cut solution was offered – the naval 2-pounder 'Pom-Pom' automatic gun. In April 1936, a meeting was held to discuss the light gun problem and two decisions were reached: first, to adopt a twin 2-pounder gun on a modified naval mounting for static use; and, second, to purchase a number of 40mm Swedish Bofors automatic guns for mobile defence of the field army.

The 2-Pounder

The 2-pounder was, in simple terms, an overgrown Maxim machine gun – belt-fed and water-cooled – although the actual operating mechanism was somewhat different. Two guns were mounted, one above the other, revolving on a baseplate anchored in concrete. Each gun fired sixty rounds per minute, the shell weighed 2lb 0.9kg), and the effective ceiling was 6,000ft. The whole equipment weighed just under eight tons – an awful lot of mounting for two small guns. Moreover, experience soon showed that the Bofors, which put exactly the same amount

of shells into the sky with one barrel and weighed about a quarter as much, was a far better weapon. No more than sixty 2-pr Mark 8 equipments were built. They were all installed in naval bases and ports, but, once ample supplies of the 40mm Bofors

The twin 2-pounder, based upon a naval pom-pom mounting, was seriously considered as the future light air-defence weapon

Fortunately, the arrival of the 40mm Bofors gun put the 2-pounder out of the race. This is the original Mark 1 gun, with later sights added. The curved chute behind the breech is a deflector, which catches the ejected cartridge case and shoots it forward, underneath the mounting

gun were assured, they were removed. By the summer of 1943, they had all been given back to the Navy for re-conversion into shipboard mountings.

The Bofors 40mm

The Bofors 40mm gun had been put on the open market in 1931, and had rapidly become popular.

Britain chose it, seeing no point in wasting time designing a gun when a perfectly good design was available off the shelf. The initial decision, of April 1937, was to purchase 100 guns and 500,000 rounds of ammunition from Bofors, followed by the negotiation of a licence to build the guns in Britain. Production took time to organize, and, as a stopgap,

The Bofors gun in action; the loader is taking a clip of four rounds to drop into the auto-loader in front of him, while a third man with more ammunition is ready to step in. Two men operating the Kerrison predictor can be seen in front of the gun

A lightweight Bofors gun stripped to the bare essentials, for use by airborne forces

more guns were purchased from Hungary and Poland (both countries had licences to manufacture).

Once manufacture got under way in Britain (and later in Canada), some variations from the original design were made. Some of these sped up production, or made it more convenient for existing machine tools. Some changes, such as improved auto-loaders or sights, improved the handling of the gun, and another, the No. 3 (or Kerrison) predictor, improved the gunnery.

The gun was not, as is sometimes alleged, an overgrown machine gun like the 2-pounder; it was an entirely conventional gun with a vertical sliding breech-block, fed by a most ingenious and reliable 'auto-loader', which was driven by the recoil forces. The breech had to be opened and loaded by hand for the first round, after which feed and fire was automatic, so long as the gun-layer kept his foot on the firing pedal, and the loader kept dropping four-round clips into the auto-loader's hopper. It fired at 120 rounds per minute, usually in short bursts.

It had a maximum ceiling of 23,600ft, although the effective ceiling was only 5,000ft, limited by the duration of the self-destroying tracer in the shell. This was a simple pyrotechnic delay device. At the end of a set time, it burned through and exploded the shell in the air, so that only fragments fell back to earth and not live unexploded shells that had missed their target. Nevertheless, this was sufficient

to deal with the intended low-flying targets. Of course, most of the shooting was done by the naked eye, so that even 5,000ft was quite high.

An Intermediate AA Gun

Efficient as the Bofors and the 3.7in guns were, they left a gap in the sky roughly between 5,000 and 10,000ft. The Bofors could deal with targets below 5,000ft, and the 3.7 could deal with them above 10,000ft. In the gap, the targets were too high for the Bofors and too fast-moving for the 3.7, which could not traverse quickly enough to track them. The 3in 20-cwt could shoot into the gap, but its rate of fire was far too slow to be effective; as the targets got faster, the 3in began falling behind.

Improved predictors, power control, radar and ammunition would, in the long term, close the gap. In 1940, this looked a long way off, and a more immediate answer was to develop a new gun purely to deal with this belt of sky – an 'intermediate AA gun'. This interesting technical challenge faced all countries at the same time; some attempted to produce a true 'intermediate' weapon, but, although some came close, none succeeded. The technology of the day was just not good enough; and for the British, the project was bedevilled by the age-old curse of trying to make one gun perform two jobs.

As usual, the British response was to see what they had in the cupboard that could be adapted; by late 1940, all that was left was a 3-pounder, under

Ordnance, QF, 40mm Gun, Bofors

The Bofors Company of Sweden had a long history of making sound, if unremarkable guns. In the late 1920s, they set about designing an anti-aircraft gun. At that time there were two groups of AA guns: those around 76mm calibre for 'deliberate' fire, and an up-and-coming 20mm or so group, for eye-shooting at low-flying attackers. Bofors decided to aim in between, with a gun that would have a respectable ceiling and a lethal shell, and would be light, handy and inexpensive. They produced their first model as the M1929, and, with a few modifications, have been at it ever since. It has become one of the classic gun designs, and it was in use by almost all the combatants during the Second World War.

The 40mm Bofors is an automatic gun, the heart of which is the 'Auto-Loader', a complex piece of machinery into which a four-round clip of ammunition is dropped. The breech is opened by hand and the auto-loader primed, after which the gun-layer aims and stamps on the firing pedal. This rams the first round, fires it, and after that it keeps on firing two shots every second until the loader stops dropping in clips or the layer lifts his foot off the pedal. The barrel was trunnioned well back, and balanced by springs, and the gun revolved on a ball-race on top of a light four-wheeled carriage. This had jacks at each end and two side-girder outriggers, also with jacks, so that they could be spread, the wheels lifted and the gun levelled by the jacks.

A wide assortment of fire-control methods were used with this gun at various times and by various people. It first appeared with a fairly simple set of metal sights using a rear crosswire and a wheel-type foresight; the Polish Army developed a 'course and speed sight', using a reflector with illuminated aiming marks. A 'corrector box' could be set with speeds up to 350mph and ranges up to 4,000 yards, and then rotated to align it with the target's course, which automatically displaced the aiming marks to provide the necessary aim-off. This was a very good sight, but it was expensive, difficult to make, and demanded a very high level of training in the gun-layer. The British abandoned it in 1940 and went back to the 'forward area sight', another wheel foresight, plus a gate-type foresight and crosswire rear sights, and then 'cartwheel' sights.

In 1944, the 'Stiffkey stick' sight (named after the AA firing practice range where it was developed) replaced all others. This was a two-man sight, set by an observer who watched the target and aligned the 'stick' with its course and set in the estimated speed. The gun-layer just had to keep the sight aligned with the target. It was also provided with power operation and receiving dials for use with a predictor (the 'Kerrison'), but most of the time it was manual operation and eye-shooting.

As well as the standard model, there were lightweight models for airborne troops, self-propelled models, naval water-cooled versions, and, in other countries, variants in 30mm and 57mm calibre. The wartime version is known as the '40/60', from the 60-calibre length of the barrel; it remained in use well into the 1960s and was then replaced, in British and other armies, by the '40/70' with a longer barrel, higher velocity and double the rate of fire. Although now replaced in British service by a guided missile, it is still in wide use around the world.

DATA (Mark 1 Gun on Mark 1 Carriage)

Calibre	40mm (1.575in)
Weight of gun and breech	427lb (193.7kg)
Total weight in action	4,368lb (1,981kg)
Barrel length	117.7 in (2.99m)
Rifling	16 grooves, increasing twist from one turn in 54 calibres to one in 30 calibres
Recoil system and length	Hydro-spring, constant, 7.87 in (200mm)
Breech mechanism	Vertical sliding block, automatic, percussion firing
Elevation	- 5 degrees to + 90 degrees
Traverse	360 degrees
Shell weight	2.0lb (907g)
Muzzle velocity	2,800ft/sec (853m/sec)
Effective ceiling	5,000ft (1,525m)
Types of projectile available	HE; AP

Ordnance, QF, 40mm Gun, Bofors continued

Their finest hour. A Bofors troop on the south coast of England during the V-1 attacks of 1944

development for the Navy, and a 57mm 6-pounder Bofors gun, developed in the mid-1930s, and more or less a scaled-up 40mm weapon. Unfortunately, the Bofors was only available in a two-barrelled naval mounting, and it was thought that, if a new mounting had to be designed and built, a new gun might just as well be designed to go with it.

The 6-pr 6-cwt Gun

In January 1941, a 6-pounder was decided upon. At that time, a number of 6-pounders were in use, particularly the 6-pr 7-cwt anti-tank gun, and the 6-pr 10-cwt coast-defence gun. However, the ballistics demanded – a ceiling of 10,000ft, and a time of flight of 5 seconds – were beyond either,

The 6-pr 6-cwt Twin 'Intermediate' anti-aircraft gun in the firing position. The automatic loading mechanism is concealed behind the gun mounting

The 6-pr 6c-wt AA gun packed up for travelling on its three-wheeled mounting

and a new gun had to be designed, with a more powerful cartridge. This became the 6-pr 6-cwt AA gun and, by the end of 1941, a twin-barrelled equipment on a three-wheeled mounting had been designed. This was built in pilot form in 1942, after which the design was changed. Among other requirements were a rate of fire of 100 rounds per minute, and a traversing speed of 25 degrees a second, and now a single-barrel automatic solution, using an automatic loading system, developed for use in a proposed self-propelled anti-tank gun, was demanded. Designs for this appeared in April 1943, but they were rejected. Fresh designs appeared in December 1943, and six pilot models were ordered – three with electrical power operation, three with hydraulic power operation.

Things were progressing in February 1944, when a new spanner was thrown into the works – General Staff decreed that the 6-pr 6-cwt gun had to be a dual-purpose AA/CD weapon, capable of being put into action on the coast, to fire at either aircraft or torpedo-boats. Scarcely had the designers taken this on board when a second decree came in June 1944 – the existing 6-pr 10-cwt coast-defence guns were to be modified to allow them to fire in the AA role.

In October 1944, the jet aircraft had become a fact of life, and the Director of Artillery demanded that the forthcoming intermediate AA gun should be able to fire at a 600mph (960k/h) target at 400 yards (370m) range; this meant a traversing speed

of 45 degrees per second, and made the existing designs useless. In December, it was decided to build twelve prototype single-gun equipments, using various power-control systems and various designs of carriage; no two were the same, as the various features were permutated in the hope of hitting on a combination that worked.

The two twin equipments built, one automatic, the other manually loaded, staggered from modification to modification. In March 1945, they were abandoned, the War Office minuting that, 'Owing to difficulties in obtaining satisfactory reliability with the 6-pr twin AA equipment, and since the designed performance is out of date . . . together with the planned development of a fully automatic single 6-pr equipment. . . the twin will not be introduced into Land Service.'

The fact is that the weapons were cumbersome, grossly unreliable. Because the auto-loading system had to be built around a breech mechanism originally designed for hand operation, the mechanical loading gear resembled one of Heath Robinson's wilder flights of imagination. It took up more space than the rest of the guns and mounting. No one was sorry to see the back of that particular design.

The end of the war came and still the 6-pr 6-cwt was in the design stage; as the post-war aircraft got faster and faster, the gun became more and more obsolescent. Eventually, the whole project was abandoned some time in the late 1940s; the proposed modification to the coast-defence gun lingered a little longer but it, too, was eventually abandoned. The idea of the intermediate gun was revived in the late 1950s as 'Red Maid', a highly automated 60mm gun designed by Oerlikon of Switzerland, but the arrival of the missile age put an end to that in a very short time.

THE USA

The 3in Guns

The Americans finished the First World War with two AA guns, both 3in calibre, but considerably different in power. Both had been developed by adapting older coast-defence guns. The first to enter service was the 3in M1917, based upon the M1903 coast gun. This was a useful and powerful gun, but it proved too powerful for a mobile mounting. For this role, the M1918 gun was produced, using the M1898 coast gun as the starting point. This used a smaller cartridge and was thus less powerful and more amenable to mounting on a mobile carriage. The only drawback was that two different rounds of ammunition were required, though, since the two designs were intended for different

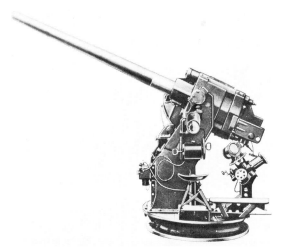

The 3in Gun M4 on Mount M3, the static version

service, this was less of a logistic problem than it seemed.

The 4.7in M1920E

The Westervelt Board had recommended the development of a powerful 4.7in gun, and work on this began in 1918, reputedly on the order of General Pershing. The M1920E was produced on a self-propelled mounting designed by Walter Christie, just before he abandoned gun mountings to concentrate on high-speed tanks. However, financial restraints caused this project to be shelved, and it was not revived for several years.

A 105mm Gun

Meanwhile, the size of the proposed 4.7in gun had led to some second thoughts, and, late in 1924, work began on a 105mm gun. This went ahead quite rapidly and, in 1927, the design was standardized as the 105mm Gun M1 on Mount M1. Further work was directed into various barrel designs, and eventually the M3 gun was standardized in 1933, the M1 and an abortive M2 being made obsolete.

The 105mm M3 was a static mounted gun which fired a 32.75lb (14.8kg) shell at 2,800ft/sec to reach a maximum ceiling of 42,000ft and an effective ceiling of 37,000ft, using the mechanical time fuze M43, which had a maximum running time of 30 seconds. This was quite commendable performance for 1933, and it is therefore surprising that only fourteen guns were ever built, in 1937–38. Most of them were installed in the fortifications of the

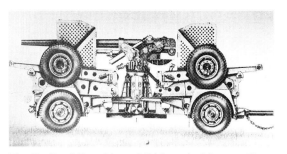

The 3in Gun M3 on Mount M2A2, packed for travelling

Panama Canal zone. The reason so few were built appears to be that, in 1938, the 90mm and 120mm guns were under development; the 90mm promised performance almost as good as the 105mm, and the 120mm was expected to perform considerably better. In view of the imminent arrival of these two guns, there seemed to be little point in perpetuating a third design which showed no appreciable advantage, so the 105mm was quietly forgotten, and made obsolete in February 1945.

Improving the 3in Guns

During the 1920–36 period, the existing 3in guns were constantly being tinkered with and improved. The M1917 gun was a satisfactory weapon as far as performance went, but the barrel was built up from a number of components; this was undesirable in an AA gun, which would require new barrel liners fairly frequently. The construction was changed to a simple tube and loose liner design, which became the M2 gun; this was found to be too flimsy and a fresh design, with a sturdier barrel and liner, became the M4 in 1928. The Mount M1917 was a simple pedestal pattern, and this had to be re-designed to take the greater weight of the M4 gun, becoming the Mount M3.

The mobile gun took rather more work, largely because of the need for a good mobile carriage. The gun was modified in the same way as the M1917, being given a loose liner, and standardized as the 3in M1 in 1927. The mount took more time, and ended up as a pedestal on a small four-wheeled platform, with four outriggers that hinged in the middle and again at the platform, so as to fold up compactly. This became the Mount M2, standardized some time in 1929.

In 1931, a fresh mounting was begun, with the intention of producing a lightweight affair on two wheels. This ended up in 1938 as the Gun T9 on Mount T4, but by that time the new 90mm design was coming close to standardization and the 3in was refused approval. Eight equipments had been built, but they were never issued for service.

Numbers of 3in guns, both static and mobile, saw action in the early days of the war in the Pacific theatre, but apart from that they remained as training weapons until completely replaced by the 90mm gun.

Light Weapons

The other development of the 1920s was in the light AA field, and involved the co-operation of the Ordnance Department, Colt's Patent Firearms Company, and John M. Browning, the noted gun designer. The object of their attention was a 37mm automatic gun. The calibre seems to have been chosen because the Army already had a 37mm 'trench cannon' of French origin, which they had adopted during the First World War. They were trying to find a weapon to replace this for ground shooting, and also to act as an air-defence weapon. Browning produced a recoil-operated gun, using a vertical sliding breech-block, and in April 1924 he demonstrated two models at Aberdeen Proving Ground.

Browning died in 1926, but the work was almost

The M2A2 mount unfolded and ready for firing

Pre-war drill on the 3in gun on M2 mount

The 105mm AA Gun M3 on Mount M1

completed and the gun was standardized in 1927, as a 'Limited Procurement Type'. In 1932, after some field tests, the potential of the weapon as a trench cannon evaporated, when the Infantry Board reported it as 'worthless'. There was more interest in developing it as an aircraft cannon and an anti-aircraft gun, so design of a suitable carriage for the latter role was now put in hand. This, the Carriage M3, was standardized in 1938, and manufacture began early the following year.

The gun was recoil-actuated and fed from a ten-round clip inserted from the side. The shell weighed 21oz, and the effective ceiling was 10,500ft, governed by a self-destroying tracer unit in the shell. It fired at a rate of 120 rounds per minute. The carriage was a four-wheeled trailer with the wheels on detachable axles; the platform was lowered to the ground and an outrigger on each side was lowered. Unlike most AA equipments, there were no levelling jacks on the platform or outriggers, but the gun pedestal was fitted into a 'levelling block', which allowed compensation for up to 10 degrees of dislevelment of the platform. It was originally entirely hand-operated, but in 1940 the British Kerrison predictor, already with the Bofors gun, was adopted as the Director M5, and the mounting was fitted with electro-hydraulic control of elevation and traverse directly from the director.

A total of 7,278 complete equipments were built.

Although the US Army later adopted the 40mm Bofors gun in large numbers, the 37mm was never entirely superseded throughout the war years; it was mostly fitted to self-propelled or trailer multiple gun mountings, in conjunction with two .50 heavy machine guns.

The 40mm Bofors

The story of the 40mm Bofors in American service began in 1937, when the US Navy attempted to purchase one from the Swedish company; for some unrecorded reason, the deal fell through and the matter was forgotten. In 1940, it was suggested that the Navy might revive its interest, and that the Army might consider the weapon with a view to standardizing on a single weapon for both services. This was something of an original (if not heretical) idea in those days. In October 1940, the Navy finally obtained a gun on a naval mounting from Britain, and in December the Army received one on the usual wheeled carriage. After examination and tests, the wheeled equipment was standardized as the 40mm Gun M1 in May 1941; the naval equipment was also taken into use at about the same time.

The Carriage M1 was the original Bofors design, and did not fit in with American methods of mass production. The Firestone Company re-designed it with a welded frame, a simplified pivot, tubular axles, electric brakes and other changes, and this was standardized in December 1941 as the Carriage M2. This was followed by the M2A1, with different gear ratios in the elevating and traversing mechanism to give faster tracking rates.

The gun was also re-designed – its screw-threads, dimensions and tolerances were altered to suit normal American manufacturing standards; these changes were incorporated into the M1 pattern without a change of number. The original ammunition provided was of British design. The Americans were not happy with a somewhat complicated British Fuze No. 251, and designed a new fuze of their own, and also a new tracer.

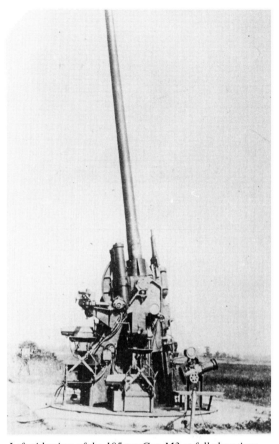

Left-side view of the 105mm Gun M3 at full elevation; this is in its emplacement on the Panama Canal and shows the fuze-setter, power cables and similar accessories that accumulate around a gun on active service

Manufacture to this design then began in the USA, and the rounds were used by both the Army and Navy.

The only significant variant produced was a lightweight two-wheeled carriage with small aircraft wheels. This variant's dimensions allowed it to be loaded into the standard C-47 Dakota transport aircraft, once the barrel and outriggers had been removed. Intended for use by airborne forces, it was also widely used in the Pacific theatre, as it took up less room in landing craft, and could be rapidly got ashore and into action in amphibious assaults.

The US 37mm AA gun M1A2 on carriage M3A2, in the firing position

The 90mm Gun M1 and Carriage M1

By the middle 1930s, a replacement for the 3in gun was seen as necessary. In 1938, the Coast Artillery Corps, responsible for air defence, asked for a gun of greater calibre, to fire a shell of not less than 21lb (9.5kg). The only restriction was that the gun had to be capable of being loaded by hand. Ballistic calculations suggested a 90mm gun firing a 24lb (11kg) shell, and work on the 90mm Gun T2 was started in June 1938, followed by the Carriage T1. The work went smoothly, and the two designs were approved and standardized in March 1940 as the Gun M1 and Carriage M1.

The 90mm gun M1 was a conventional design with vertical sliding breech-block. It fired a 23.4lb (10.65kg) shell at 2,700ft/sec to reach an effective ceiling of 33,800ft, with a 30-second fuze, and could reach a rate of fire of fifteen rounds per minute when fitted with a spring rammer.

The carriage was of an unusual design, with two dual-wheels. Three of the outriggers folded around the pedestal, while the fourth acted as the connection to the towing vehicle, and the wheels were completely removed when the gun was put into position. A static mount was also produced, at the request of the coast artillery, which allowed the gun to function in a dual role for air and coast defence.

The 90mm M1 was a very good weapon, but rather slow to get into action. The Chiefs of Staff decided that they required a gun capable of a faster deployment in emergency, and able to engage ground and sea targets – a 'triple-threat gun'. In September 1942, development of a new model began. In the gun, there was very little change, but the carriage was entirely different.

The new carriage design showed a cruciform mounting with four wheels, outriggers, folding platforms and folding shields. It was fitted for hand or remote power control of traverse and elevation, and provided with a mechanical fuze-setter and rammer, driven by electric motors. This took the form of rubber rollers set into the breech ring; the gunner presented the round to the breech, where the rollers were turning slowly. The rollers moved inwards, increased their speed, and pulled the shell forward, so that the fuze entered the fuze-setter, set into the breech ring. After the fuze had been set, the jaws of the fuze-setter opened wide and the roller speed accelerated, so as to propel the round into the chamber. The breech closed and the gun fired. The Fuze Setter and Rammer M20 gave a fixed dead time of 2.6 seconds, and brought the rate of fire up to twenty-seven rounds per minute.

The 120mm Gun M1

The last addition to the AA arsenal was the 4.7in gun, which had been shelved in the 1920s. The project was revived in 1938, and specifications were issued in June 1939. Technology had progressed since 1924 and, instead of simply pulling out the old drawings, a completely new weapon was designed; the result was introduced as the 4.7in Gun M1 in late 1940. To conform with later standards, it was re-named as the 120mm Gun M1 in January 1944.

The gun was entirely conventional and so was the carriage, with its cruciform platform, with outriggers, travelling on two dual-wheeled axles. It was entirely power-operated, and had a fuze-setter and rammer that used a swinging arm to punch the round into the chamber. The shell and cartridge were separate items and were dropped on to the loading tray. The rammer arm then supported the base of the cartridge, while the fuze-setter moved down over the shell and set the fuze. The setter

withdrew, the tray swung down to line up with the breech, and the arm swung, propelling the cartridge and thus ramming the shell. The tray and rammer then swung up again out of the recoil path, and the gun fired. With a well-drilled detachment, it could fire at twelve rounds per minute; the shell weighed 50lb and the cartridge 48lb (21.8kg), so this meant shifting half a ton of ammunition from the ground to the loading tray every minute. The shell left the gun at 3,100ft/sec and could reach an effective ceiling of 47,400ft; the maximum ceiling was 57,450ft.

Only 550 of these guns were made; except for a few that were sent to the Panama Canal zone, and four that arrived in Northern Ireland and were never used, they all stayed inside the USA. It was felt that the field armies had adequate protection from their

The 37mm gun in training, 1940. The man at the right is pushing a clip of ammunition into the loading tray

Gun, 90mm, AA

A 90mm AA Gun M1A1 on Mount M1A1, in march order

Like Britain, America had settled on 3in as their AA gun calibre and, also like Britain, by the early 1930s they realized that something with more authority was needed. If a near miss was all that could be hoped for, the bigger the shell, the less near the miss had to be. In 1938, the Coast Artillery Board (responsible for AA artillery) demanded a gun firing a shell weighing at least 21lb, the upper limit of calibre to be determined by the fact that the gun had to be loaded by hand. When all the sums had been done, the result was a 90mm gun firing a 24lb shell, and on 9 June 1938 development of the 90mm Gun T2 was authorized. Approval for development of the Mounting T1 was given on 18 August. Work moved quickly and smoothly, and both were standardized as the 90mm M1 on 21 March 1940.

The M1 was a quite conventional gun on a rather unusual four-outrigger mounting, which folded up around a single axle with dual wheels. The most prominent and recognizable feature was the perforated metal platforms folded up alongside the gun in the travelling mode. One of the outriggers acted as the towing connection, and the entire unit was quite compact, but it was not the fastest gun of its kind into action.

In May 1941, the Gun M1A1 and Mount M1A1 were standardized; the gun had a few small modifications to the breech area in order to accommodate a spring rammer, while the mounting had remote power control equipment added. The spring rammer turned out to be less of a good idea than had been hoped, and it was usually either disconnected or taken off altogether. Although approved in 1941, the M1A1 equipment had gone into production in late 1940 ahead of approval; by the time of the North African invasion in late 1942, more than 2,000 were in use, and it remained in service until well after the war.

The only defect with the M1A1 was that it was relatively slow getting into action. The Chiefs of Staff decided that a gun capable of firing at ground targets and sea targets would also be an advantage, so the Gun M2 on Mount M2 appeared in May 1943. The gun was the same as the M1A1, except for the method of attaching the breech ring, and the removal of the various modifications to take the spring rammer, plus the incorporation into the breech of parts of a new roller-rammer. The mount was considerably altered; it was now on a four-wheel carriage, so that it could be got into action much faster, and it had ten degrees of depression, to allow it to fire at sea-coast targets. The roller-rammer boosted the rate of fire to twenty-seven rounds per minute.

As well as relying on the 90mm M2 as a stopgap coast-defence weapon, a proper coast pedestal mounting was provided, known as the Mount M3. This was the usual sort of shielded pedestal, developed in 1941-1943. By the time it had been perfected, however, there was little need for additional coast-defence guns, and it is unlikely that many were made or emplaced.

DATA (Gun M1A1 on Mounting M1A1)

Calibre	90mm (3.54in)
Weight of gun and breech	2,445lb (1,109 kg)
Total weight in action	1,7714lb (8,035kg)
Barrel length	186.15in (4.72m)
Rifling	32 grooves, right-hand, one turn in 32 calibres
Recoil system and length	Hydro-pneumatic, variable, 26 to 44in (66 to 111cm)
Breech mechanism	Vertical sliding block, semi-automatic, percussion firing
Elevation	0 degrees to + 80 degrees
Traverse	360 degrees
Shell weight	23.40lb (10.61 kg)
Muzzle velocity	2,700ft/sec (823m/sec)
Effective ceiling	33,820ft (10,308m)
Types of projectile available	HE; APC/HE

90mm guns, and the 120mm would only be required if the enemy developed aircraft capable of reaching the USA. During the Cold War, a number were deployed in Europe.

The Proximity Fuze

There was one more development, which did not reach completion during the war, but which must be mentioned because of its origins in the wartime advances of electronic technology. This was the 75mm T22 gun, which came into existence because of the development of the proximity fuze.

Anti-aircraft fire was based upon the use of high-explosive shells fitted with time fuzes, and the running time of the fuze was a highly critical figure in gunnery calculations. However, even the best clockwork fuzes were prone to error; they were mass-produced clock mechanisms, generally assumed to have a margin of error of about half a per cent. In other words, if the fuze was set at 28 seconds, it could err by 0.14 seconds either side of its predicted point of burst. If the shell was travelling at 2,000ft/sec, this meant a spread of 280ft, plus or minus. As the average AA shell in the 3.7/90mm class had a lethal burst area of 50ft, some of the shells would obviously burst too far from the target to do any damage. The only answer was to fire as many rounds as possible, in the hope that some of them would burst closer to the target than others.

A 90mm M1A1 gun in action in Iceland, 1942

When the British began work on AA radar, the scientists were horrified to learn that there was such a thing as the 'zone of the gun' – which represented a random error of the shell's flight – as well as a 'zone of the fuze'; this made gunnery seem to them a highly speculative business. One scientist suggested that, if a radar receiver was put in the

Setting the fuze on a 90mm shell before loading

Ground firing with a 90mm gun in Belgium, 1944

fuze, it would pick up the echo from the gun-directing radar pointed at the target. Fixing a circuit, so that the fuze would respond when the signal reached a strength indicating the target within fifty feet, and detonate the shell, would eliminate this fuze error, and the need to calculate fuze lengths, and set them. However, the radar echo was very weak, and the sort of circuit needed could not, at that time (1938), be put inside a shell fuze. (Indeed, it would hardly fit inside a small truck at that stage of its development.) The idea was reluctantly abandoned.

The next idea was to made a small and simple radio transmitter inside the fuze, together with a simple receiver, which would respond when the signal emitted by the fuze was reflected back to it by the target. In theory, this was much simpler and cheaper, although miniaturized valves and other electronic components would need to be developed, as would some sort of power supply to drive the radio. There was little chance of that happening in Britain in 1939–40, when every radio component manufacturer was already working overtime

90mm M2 guns on a firing range in Germany in 1956

122

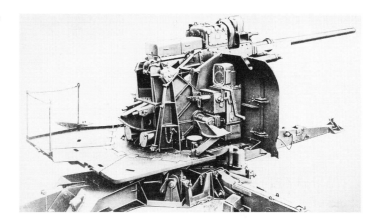

Rear view of the 90mm M2 gun in firing position. The apparatus above the breech is the fuze-setter/rammer machinery

producing radar and radio equipment.

In August 1940, the Tizard Mission, a body of eminent scientists and experts, went to the USA to introduce a number of technological wonders to the Americans. Most famously, these included the cavity magnetron, which made centimetric radar a practical possibility, and also among them was the idea for the radio proximity fuze. The Americans agreed to develop it; the US Navy took over the development, and farmed it out to Kodak, who then contracted Exide (for the battery) and Sylvania (for the valves). The project was under the control of Section V of the US Navy Bureau of Ordnance, and they allotted it the code letter 'T'; the device became the 'VT' fuze. Most people thought this stood for 'variable time', and they were not disabused of this, since it was an acceptable name, which did not suggest an electronic item. The first fuzes were produced early in 1943 and saw their first success in June, when the USS *Helena* shot down a Japanese aircraft. They went on to more success against the V1 flying bomb campaign against London, and then were adopted for field artillery.

The 75mm T22

Once the proximity fuze was in service, it became apparent that it produced more accurate fire, and also a higher rate of fire, because there was no fuze setting and, hence, no dead time. From this came the idea of a gun without any fuze setting device, but capable of the highest possible rate of fire. Moreover, other electronic advances made it feasible to think about giving each gun its own radar and predictor. The 75mm T22 was the result.

The calibre of 75mm was chosen because it was necessary to use a relatively compact round of ammunition for the automatic loading system. The proximity fuze was, at that stage of its development, a bulky device that occupied a much greater portion of the inside of the shell than previous fuzes, leaving space for less explosive. The minimum acceptable calibre for an effective shell was 75mm, and a complete round of ammunition for this gun was just about the optimum size for the loading system envisaged. The trouble was that this combination of round and gun could not achieve a good enough muzzle velocity to give the weapon the performance that was needed.

The development of the gun was relatively easy, and by January 1945 a prototype had been tested. The development of the mounting, however, was a very different matter. It was to be a cruciform-type mounting of the normal AA type, but on the rotating gun platform would be a centimetric tracking radar, an optical tracker, and a predictor. Behind the gun would be two rotating drums, each containing ten rounds, feeding alternately to a central rammer to give a rate of fire of forty-five rounds per minute. This was stretching current technology to its limit, and the equipment was far from being finished

The 4.7in AA Gun M1920E on a self-propelled mounting, designed by Walter Christie before he began designing his better-known tanks

The 120mm M1 gun, in march order; note that the barrel has been disconnected from the recoil system and pulled back to avoid excess whip, and distribute the weight between the wheels

The 120mm gun M1 in firing position, but without the fuze-setter/rammer

Another view of the 120mm gun in travelling mode; the cage-like piece at the top is the cartridge guide for the rammer

FUZE SETTER CLUTCH

FUZE SETTER SPEED REDUCER

CAM BRAKE

FUZE SETTER CAM

FUZE SETTER

MOTOR

CHAMBER

CLUTCH CONTROL HANDLE

RAMMER ARM

RAMMER CLUTCH

SHIFTER HANDLE

LOADING TRAY

PROJECTILE

DRUM CAM

CARTRIDGE CASE

DRUM CAM BRAKE

RA PD 108098A

The mechanics of the fuze-setter/rammer on the 120mm gun M1. The rammer arm unit pivots; it starts with the shell aligned with the fuze-setter, which slides back and sets the fuze. It then returns, the unit pivots into the position seen here, and the rammer arm delivers an uppercut to the cartridge case and rams the entire round at one move

An American Bofors guarding an airstrip in the South Pacific, 1944

The 75mm 'Skysweeper' as it finally appeared in the early 1950s. The seated corporal is operating the radar tracker, the antenna dish of which can be seen beneath the barrel. Just behind the standing man is the cage-like structure of the rotary magazine

Firing a 120mm Gun M1 on a range in Germany in the 1950s. The loader has just dropped the cartridge into the rammer unit

when the war ended. At this time, the pressure eased, some basic research was done, and the equipment finally got into service in the early 1950s as the M51 'Skysweeper'. Even then, it fell short of expectations, particularly in the matter of velocity, since the service gun could produce only 2,600ft/sec. As soon as a workable missile appeared, the M51 was retired.

RUSSIA

The 76 mm M1931 and the M1938

The usual cloud of uncertainty surrounds the story of Russian AA gun development. It is known that a 76.2mm AA gun was developed during the First World War, and presumably remained in service through the 1920s. The first improved gun on which there is data was the 7.62mm M1931, a design which appears to have had its roots in a Vickers commercial pattern developed for export in the 1920s. It used a two-wheeled cruciform carriage with the usual outriggers. It fired a 6.6kg shell at 813m/sec to a

The arrival of the Bofors gun in American service; training in 1942 – note the difference in dress and the absence of rifles

A Soviet 37mm M1939 gun in Aberdeen Proving Ground, USA

claimed maximum ceiling of 30,500ft; presumably, the effective ceiling would have been about 25,000ft. It remained in service throughout the Second World War, when numbers were captured by the Germans and taken into use until they wore out, or the captured ammunition stocks were exhausted.

The M1931 was brought up to date, by being fitted with a more modern four-wheeled carriage and having its sighting system improved, and the result went into service as the 76.2mm Model 1938. It still used the same gun and ammunition as the M1931, so the performance was the same, although it is probable that the rate of fire was a little better. As with the M1931, it was used throughout the war, and large numbers went into German hands. Instead of being scrapped when their ammunition ran out, many of these were re-barrelled in 88mm calibre, and used standard German 88mm Flak 18 ammunition.

A Soviet 37mm gun in Konigsberg in 1945

76mm Anti-Aircraft Gun M1938

As usual with Soviet equipment, there are no precise dates or specification details available to give an accurate history of the 76mm AA Gun M1938. It is known that it was the last of a series of 76mm guns that dated back to 1915, when, as usual for the period, an existing coast-defence gun was adapted to fire upwards. This pattern was replaced by a new model in 1931, a design that used a single-axle carriage, which was similar to guns then being designed and sold commercially by Vickers of Britain, Schneider of France, and other firms. (The last of this breed was, in fact, the American 90mm M1.)

A 76.2mm M1931 gun mounted on a motor truck in the defence of Moscow in 1941

The mounting was seen to be the weak part of the design, and it was re-designed into a two-axle model with four outriggers. The sights were also improved. It may be that experience in the Spanish Civil War, when the German 'advisers' demolished the tanks of the Russian 'advisers' by using their 88mm anti-aircraft guns, led the Soviets to ensure that adequate ground-fire sights were provided, as well as armour-piercing ammunition. Certainly, there are wartime photographs of this gun in action against ground targets that bear out this theory.

The M1938 was the last of its calibre; as in other countries, the Soviets decided that something with a better terminal effect was necessary, and moved up to the 85mm calibre for their next design, which appeared in 1939. The 76mm model continued to serve throughout the war; it may have been obsolescent, but it was still capable of doing damage.

DATA

Calibre	76.2 mm (3.0 in)
Weight of gun and breech	448kg (988lb)
Total weight in action	4,300kg (9,481lb)
Barrel length	3.888m (153in)
Rifling	32 grooves, right-hand twist, one turn in 25 calibres
Recoil system and length	Hydro-pneumatic, variable, 70 to 115cm (27 to 45in)
Breech mechanism	Vertical sliding block, semi-automatic, percussion
Elevation	- 3 degrees to + 82 degrees
Traverse	360 degrees
Shell weight	6.5kg (14.54lb)
Muzzle velocity	815m/sec (2,673ft/sec)
Effective ceiling	9,500m (31,160ft)
Types of projectile available:	HE; AP/HE; APCR; shrapnel

The 85mm Guns

Even as the M1938 went into production, it was obvious that something better had to be provided, because the aeroplanes were getting faster and higher. Work on an 85mm gun had begun some time in 1936, and the 85mm M1939 duly appeared just in time for the war, although it was not in service in great numbers until about 1942. It was a good design – large numbers are in use around the world today, and the gun itself became a versatile tank and anti-tank gun. The usual sort of four-wheeled cruciform mounting was used, with hand operation, although in post-war years it was given power operation and radar control. It fired a 9.2kg shell at

Soviet 85mm M1939 gun at Aberdeen Proving Ground

800m/sec to reach an effective ceiling of 25,000 feet at 70 degrees elevation, and had a rate of fire of about fifteen rounds per minute.

The M1939 was later improved to produce the 85mm M1944. This had the chamber bored out, to take a more powerful cartridge, the recoil system strengthened, and the gun fitted with a muzzle brake, so that the performance was improved. Firing the same 9.2kg shell, it could now reach a muzzle velocity of 900m/sec, and an effective ceiling of 30,800ft. This also stayed in service in post-war years, although it was largely replaced in the Soviet Army in the late 1940s by 100mm weapons and handed out to other Warsaw Pact armies.

The 105mm Gun

The largest Russian wartime AA gun was a 105mm weapon apparently built in the Leningrad arsenal, on a static mounting for the protection of cities and vulnerable points. It had a 60-calibre barrel, fired a 33lb (15kg) shell at 3,050ft/sec to reach a maximum ceiling of 43,500ft, and had a rate of fire of about

A wartime picture of an 85mm M1939 gun being used as an anti-tank gun, somewhere on the Eastern Front in 1943

The Soviet 85mm M1944 was a slightly improved version of the M1939, with a shield added

twelve rounds per minute. The few pictures of this gun show it to be quite conventional, except for an unusual pair of balancing springs alongside the barrel, rather like the 152mm field gun.

Light Weapons

In the light air-defence field, the Russians had only two guns: the 37mm Model 1939 and the 25mm Model 1940. Both of these appear to have been copied from Bofors designs, the 37mm from the well-known 40mm pattern, and the 25mm from an original 25mm Bofors design which was, in most respects, simply a scaled-down version of the 40mm. The 25mm weapon appeared in three versions – the M1939, M1940 and M1941 – the difference between them appearing to be in manufacturing detail.

The most common of the three was the M1940, a Bofors look-alike, with the same sort of four-wheeled carriage with two outriggers. It was clip-fed, firing a shell weighing about 9oz at 2,990ft/sec, to reach a maximum ceiling of 7,925ft. It is likely that the self-destruction element in the shells operated well before that level was reached.

The 37mm M1939 is another remarkable survivor, with hundreds still in use throughout Africa and the Far East, and some other areas. This fired a 1.6lb (0.75kg) shell at 2,885ft/sec, to a claimed maximum ceiling of 19,600ft. The effective ceiling, governed by the self-destruction time of the shell, was about 10,000ft. It used a Bofors-type five-round clip, and could reach a rate of fire of about 170 rounds per minute. It was unusual in the light AA field in that it was provided with an armour-piercing round for ground use, capable of defeating 46mm of armour at 500m (545 yards) range.

5   Anti-Tank Artillery

A 'PURE' ANTI-TANK GUN?

The anti-tank gun was born out of the Second World War, although it had its roots in the First World War. The concept of a dedicated gun for dealing with tanks first appeared in 1917–18. However, until the late 1930s, the tank was a fairly easy target – as far as defeating its armour was concerned – and very little serious thought went into the subject. Any consideration of such a weapon revolved around lightweight weapons that could be manhandled by the infantry. In 1936–39, there was a school of thought that maintained that the tank was no longer a threat since it had been mastered by the anti-tank gun.

With the rapid improvement in tank armour and performance after 1939, it soon became apparent that pre-war ideas were out-dated. Some highly specialized weapons – and, more particularly, ammunition – had to be developed in order to counter the armoured threat. However, the thinking was still on conventional lines, and the answer to a heavier tank was always a heavier gun; in the long run, this approach sounded the death-knell for a 'pure' anti-tank gun. In order to defeat the massive armour of the 1944–45 tanks, a conventional gun had to be so big that it became a totally impractical weapon, too big to manhandle or conceal.

What saved the day for the gun was not gun design, but ammunition design, and in particular two innovations – the shaped charge, and the tungsten sub-projectile. Both these had a subsequent effect upon gun design, leading to a divergance from the conventional, and producing some interesting equipment. Without an appreciation of how the ammunition developed, the development of the guns becomes somewhat opaque.

AMMUNITION

The art of knocking holes in armour plate did not begin with the tank in 1917, but with the iron-clad warship in the 1860s. By the First World War, the demands of naval and coast-defence gunnery had brought it to a high degree of perfection. There were two types of projectile: armour-piercing (AP) shell and armour-piercing shot. The difference was that shell was hollow and carried a charge of explosive, while shot was solid steel.

Shell

The theory behind the shell was that the hardened tip would smash through the plate and the shell would shoulder its way through, widening the hole; meanwhile, the shock of the initial impact would have begun the operation of a base fuze, which, ideally, would complete its function just as the base of the shell passed through the armour and into the warship's vitals. At that point, the fuze would detonate the explosive filling and shatter the shell, wrecking the internals of the ship with blast and fragmentation, and also causing serious damage to the crew.

Shot

Shot simply smashed its way through the plate and sped on its way, shattering whatever it came across inside the ship. Any damage done after the penetration was more or less random.

The differences reflect the two views of the attack of armour; one approach is to attack the protection, while the other is to attack what is being protected. This is a distinction frequently lost sight of, even today.

Problems

The AP shell often did not work precisely as the designers wanted it to; notably, the fuze would detonate part-way through the armour (if it was thick), or after passing through both sides of the armoured vessel (if it was thin). The compression of the shell body as it squeezed through the armour plate (which could be 10–15in thick, or even thicker, on a major warship) sometimes caused the fuze to pop out like a cork out of a squeezed bottle, and before it had been able to detonate the explosive.

Another drawback was that, in order to have the necessary weight and strength to smash through heavy armour, the shell had only a small capacity for explosive – around 2.5 to 3.5 per cent of its weight. (A conventional high-explosive shell would contain anything from 8 to 15 per cent.) The smaller percentage was tolerable in a 15in naval shell weighing 1,500lb (681.8kg), which then contained 45lb (20.5kg) of explosive. However, in a 3in anti-tank shell weighing 15lb (6.8kg), the HE content was just 7oz. Moreover, the conventional shell would be filled with some lively substance such as TNT or RDX; the AP shell had to have a relatively insensitive explosive, which would survive the immense shock of initial impact without detonating, but which would infallibly detonate when it received the lesser impulse from the base fuze.

By adopting AP shot, all these complications were avoided. Half a ton of pointed steel was simply dumped on to the enemy ship, in the hope that sheer momentum would do some damage; it usually did.

Face-Hardened Armour

There were two types of armour: homogenous or face-hardened, also called 'carburised' or 'Harveyised'. Homogenous was of a similar density and hardness all the way through, and the skill of the armour-maker was to get the right degree of toughness. If it was too tough, it was liable to shatter like a piece of glass when struck a heavy blow; if it was not tough enough, the AP shot or shell would simply slide through it. Investigations led to the idea of face-hardening; a slab of homogenous armour would be laid in a special furnace, its upper face covered with some heavily carbon-bearing material. The whole lot would be brought up to white heat and maintained there for hours, or even days, after which it was gradually cooled. The process caused carbon to be absorbed into the face of the plate, making it extremely hard. In fact, it was so hard that it would have been brittle, if it were not for the fact that the remainder of the thickness was still the original tough homogenous armour; this now acted as a support and backing, preventing the face-hardened zone from shattering.

The 'Penetrating Cap'

The answer to face-hardening was the 'penetrating cap', a mild steel cap placed over the front end of the AP projectile. The interior surface of the cap was shaped, so that it did not touch the tip of the projectile; on impact, the blow was transferred to the shoulders of the projectile rather than being concentrated on the tip. At the impact velocity and force involved, the cap was virtually melted; it supported the projectile long enough to allow the tip to make an impression on the face-hardening, after which it became a form of lubricant, assisting the penetration, so that the face-hardening was defeated and the projectile began cutting its way through the softer support. The only drawback was that the ideal shape for the cap was not an ideal shape for cleaving through the air; an additional light metal 'ballistic cap' was sometimes fitted in front of the penetrating cap, to improve the projectile's flight characteristics.

Krupp confounded this design in the 1890s with the invention of 'Krupp Cemented Plate', simply face-hardened armour applied back to front, so that the AP projectile struck the tough homogenous section of the plate first and then, having been slowed up by that, struck the reverse side of the face-hardening, by which time it no longer had sufficient momentum to pierce it.

Penetration

The question of penetration, and how it was defined, is interesting. Imagine a tank presenting a side view to the gun, so that the shot strikes the armour at a perfect right-angle. If the armour plate is 100mm thick, the shot has to go through 100mm. If it does so, its performance is '100mm, at *x* range, at normal', in other words, with the shot arriving square on to the target plate. At 500 yards, for example, the shorthand for this would be '100/500/0 degrees'; in British terminology, the angle of arrival was measured from a line at right-angles to the target. (On the continent at that time, the angle was measured from the plane of the target face, so that the British 0 degrees was a German or French 90 degrees. Today, Britain has conformed to the continental system, for the sake of NATO standardization.)

However, shots rarely strike the plate at a perfect right-angle; more often than not, the line of fire causes the shot to strike obliquely, and even if the gun is at right-angles to the tank, the designer of the tank will probably have sloped the armour. Once this happens, the conditions change. If a shot strikes at 30 degrees from the normal, its path through the armour is more than 100 mm. The calculation is 100mm divided by the cosine of the angle of attack: 100/Cos 30 = 115, so in reality the shot has to pass through 115mm of steel to penetrate a 100mm-thick plate. The steeper the angle, the higher the values: at 60 degrees, the shot has to go through 200mm of armour. The shorthand now reads '100/500/30 degrees', meaning that the gun can defeat 100mm of armour at 500 yards range at a 30-degree angle of attack. (Remember that during the war years, the British 30 degrees was 60 degrees on the continent.)

Tank Warfare

The shell manufacturers developed alloy-steel shot and shell bodies of exceptional hardness, as well as superior caps and ingenious fuzes, and, one way and another, they could generally defeat any armour, provided they could get a big enough gun close enough. When the tank first appeared on the

'My object all sublime, I shall achieve in time. . .' It is astonishing what a few well-directed pounds of steel will do if thrown hard enough

battlefield, there was a significant amount of expertise ready to be tapped and applied.

In fact, that expertise of the late nineteenth century was hardly relevant in the First World War; the tanks of 1916–18 could be penetrated by little more than an AP rifle or machine-gun bullet, while the impact of a common high-explosive shell against the outside was sufficient to put them out of action.

Small Anti-Tank Guns

The development of infantry anti-tank guns in the 1930s led to a revival of interest in AP shot and shell, and investigations were begun to see if there might be something the nineteenth-century engineers had overlooked. The problem was that the contemporary anti-tank gun was seen as a small-calibre weapon, because the tanks were not very thickly armoured, and the foot soldiers had to push or pull the guns into action. Given a calibre of 37 to 40mm, therefore, an AP shell with a 2.5 per cent explosive content was getting very close to an inert AP shot, as far as target effect was concerned.

The Spanish Civil War, in which a variety of light tanks and armoured cars appeared, and were confronted by an equal variety of small anti-tank guns, led people to draw conclusions about tank warfare. One conclusion was that the anti-tank gun was the master of the tank. In common with most other theories connected with the Spanish Civil War, this one was all wrong when applied to anything other than the rather unreal conditions that had held in Spain. However, it was easier to accept it, and all the combatants in 1939 lined up with 37mm to 45mm anti-tank guns, which could be easily pushed around by a handful of men, and easily concealed. To be fair, these guns could make holes in virtually any tank of 1939; their perforation performance averaged around 2in of homogenous armour at 500 yards.

Achieving Increased Velocity

Of course, when the tank people started to complain about holes in their tanks, the designers got to work;

the next generation of tanks was thicker, and some of them had face-hardened armour, and soon the gunners began to complain that their shot and shell were bouncing off the tanks. So the gun designers got to work and designed bigger guns to throw bigger shot at faster velocities, to give the armour a fiercer blow. At that point, things began to go wrong. It was discovered that the velocity could not be increased indefinitely; there came a point when the impact of the shot (or shell) upon the armour was so intense, the shot itself shattered before it could start to bore through the armour. This had never been seen before; long-range engagements with warships meant that the shot landed at a relatively low velocity, certainly much lower than that achieved in a short-range shot at a tank.

The first answer was to adopt capped shot, which spread the impact over the shoulders of the projectile. However, this just moved the critical velocity upwards by a small amount, after which the shatter re-appeared. It was essential to find something harder than steel and make the shot out of that. The solution seemed to be tungsten carbide, but that brought its own problem: tungsten carbide is 1.6 times as dense as steel. The same size of shot would weigh 10lb (4.5kg) in steel and 16lb (7.25kg) in tungsten. A 16lb (7.25kg) shot needs more pressure to move it, but the amount of pressure that can be applied is limited by the strength of the gun, so that the 16lb (7.25kg) shot could only be fired at about half the velocity of the steel shot.

Unconventional Designs

At this point it was realized that there was no mileage in making a shot out of tungsten, as long as conventional ammunition design techniques were applied. It was time to try some unconventional designs.

The problem, stated mathematically, was as follows: to obtain high velocity in the gun, a shot with small weight in comparison to its diameter is needed, or a low value of w/d^3 (weight divided by the cube of the diameter). To get good flight characteristics and high velocity outside the gun, a high value is needed, that is, a shot that is heavy in comparison to its diameter. How to start with one, and end up with the other?

The Germans achieved this aim by using a gun with a tapering bore and designing a shot with a small-diameter tungsten core, supported in a full-calibre soft metal 'skirt'. The bore at the chamber was 2.8cm; at the muzzle it had reduced to 2cm, and the shot had been squeezed down to fit. When loaded, the w/d^3 ratio was 5.96; as it left the muzzle, it was 16.4. This had another advantage: if the gas pressure behind the shot remained constant, but the diameter of the shot decreased, the pressure per square inch on the base of the shot went up, and so did the velocity.

Britain took a different route to the same answer, with its development of the 'Armour-Piercing Discarding Sabot' (APDS) shot. They put the tungsten core inside a full-calibre light-alloy 'sabot' or shoe, and designed it so that the sabot split and dropped off as it left the gun, leaving the core to fly on alone. Here, the w/d^3 figure as loaded was 8, and after it left the muzzle and got rid of the sabot it went up to 40. The combination tungsten and alloy shot was just over half the weight of a standard 6lb (2.75kg) steel shot, so it went up the bore at a satisfactory velocity. Because of its change of shape, it maintained that velocity to the target where, because of the tungsten, it punched holes through 4in of plate at 1,000 yards range.

The Shaped Charge

The alternative route to defeating armour was to rely upon science rather than brute force, to deliver a charge of high explosive on to the armour and use the energy of the explosive to make the hole. An ordinary HE shell was no use for this task, since it merely detonated on the outside of the armour, and did relatively little damage, unless it was a very large shell hitting a small tank. The explosive force had to be directed, and one way of doing this was with the 'shaped charge' or 'hollow charge'. This had begun as a laboratory trick in the 1880s and had been gradually refined until, by the late 1930s, it

offered a useful technology.

The theory behind this technology was as follows. A cylinder of explosive has one end hollowed out into a cone or hemisphere, and this cavity is lined with some dense material – for example, copper or glass. The hollow face is placed in contact with a piece of steel, the charge is detonated at its rear end, deforming the lining into a high-speed jet of explosive gas and molten metal, which has sufficient power to blast its way through the metal. If the charge is set a small distance away from the armour – about twice the charge's diameter – and then fired, the jet has more space to gather speed and form itself, and the penetration will be even deeper. Such a device will pierce armour plate with the greatest of ease, and, as an added advantage, velocity will have no effect upon the result. The projectile can be fired at 1,000 feet per second, or it can be placed in position by hand; the result is the same, since it is entirely dependent upon the explosive, not the method of delivery.

The shaped charge become the second significant method of killing tanks (even though it did have its drawbacks), and, by and large, has remained so. The projectiles (and missiles) in use today have improved beyond what could have been imagined in 1944, but the principles remain the same.

BRITAIN

Throughout the Second World War, the development of guns and ammunition in the anti-tank effort was to continue to be complementary, laying a solid foundation for subsequent research.

The 2-Pounder

The standard (and only) anti-tank gun of the British Army in 1939 was the Vickers-designed 2-pounder gun. It has become obligatory to deride this weapon (and its infantry companion, the .55in Boys rifle), but the fact is that when war broke out, the 2-pounder was more than capable of holding its own against any tank in the German Army. It could out-

*The prototype of the 2-pounder gun;
this basic design was adhered to,
although there were several changes
of detail*

perform any other anti-tank gun of comparable calibre in the world, defeating 42mm of homogenous armour at 1,000 yards at a 30-degree angle of attack. In addition, it was certainly the best-designed gun of its kind.

In the first place, the 2-pounder gun was designed as a tank gun; in view of the need for economy, it was accepted by the Director of Artillery in October 1934, although with some misgivings as to the effectiveness of a 40mm piercing shell. Competitive contracts were given to Vickers and to Woolwich Arsenal to produce an equipment.

As in the early 1930s, the prime requirements for

an anti-tank gun, once sufficient penetration was assured, were a firm platform and a fast, wide and smooth traverse, to allow rapid switching between targets and tracking of a moving target. The 2-pounder Mark 9 on Carriage Mark 1, designed by Vickers, was given a three-legged platform, one leg of which formed the towing trail, and the other two folded up for travelling. A sprung axle carried two wheels on brackets, so that once the gun was positioned, the three legs were placed on the ground and the wheels swung up off the ground. Screw jacks at the end of the three platform legs could then be operated to level the equipment. The gun could then traverse through 360 degrees, to cope with

*The 2-pounder ready for towing, with
two of its trail legs folded up*

targets from any direction; the traversing mechanism had a two-speed gear, allowing a very fast movement to pick up targets, and a slower one for following and aiming at moving targets. On top of it all was a superlative telescope sight.

The Vickers design had been accepted since it was first past the post, and could be produced reasonably quickly. A limited number was ordered and issues began in 1936. However, the Woolwich design was found to be easier and cheaper to manufacture and became the Mark 2 carriage, first issued late in 1938. This had much the same features as the Mark 1, but differed in that the wheels were removed when it was placed on its ground platform. Both models could also be fired from their wheels, although this restricted the amount of traverse.

The 6-Pounder

Astute soldiers realized that tank design was moving forward all the time and, sooner rather than later, the 2-pounder would be out-matched. Even as the first 2-pounders entered service, the design department at Woolwich Arsenal had been given instructions to prepare its replacement. In 1938, the design for a 57mm 6-pounder appeared. In 1939, a prototype had been built and test-fired, after which

the designs were sealed and put away ready for the day when they would be needed.

When the army took stock after the Dunkirk evacuation, it found that 509 2-pounders had been left behind in France; there were only 167 anti-tank guns left in Britain, and it was imperative to get more manufactured in order to re-equip formations and also meet the demands of a rapidly expanding army. The question was whether to put the 6-pounder or the 2-pounder into production. The latter was chosen, since production was running and the troops were familiar with the gun; putting the 6-pounder into production would have meant a delay of six or eight months before the first guns appeared, after which would come the problem of re-training. With Hitler's Wehrmacht standing on the French cliffs and viewing the British coast through their binoculars, a wait of six to eight months was out of the question.

Nevertheless, the Director of Artillery placed an order for 400 6-pounders in June 1940, on the understanding that production would commence only when the immediate demand for 2-pounders had been satisfied. The result was that the first guns appeared from production in November 1941; within six months, they were coming out of the factories at a rate of 1,500 a month.

The 6-pounder of 2.244in (57mm) calibre had

Front view of the 2-pounder in the firing position

Rear view of the 2-pounder in the firing position; note the massive sight bracket and large telescope

been a service gun since the 1880s in one form or another; this version entered service as the '6-pounder 7-cwt Mark 1', its weight part of the nomenclature in order to distinguish it from the many other 6-pounders that had gone before or were still in service. The gun was mounted on a two-wheeled, split-trail carriage which allowed it 45 degrees of traverse to either side. Its theoretical maximum range was 5,500 yards, although it was never fired at such a range. The more important performance figure was its penetration of armour. With the standard 6lb (2.75kg) steel shot, it could defeat 74mm of armour at 1,000 yards at a 30-degree angle of attack. This was to improve

progressively as the ammunition specialists got to work.

The 6-pounder soon made a name for itself – indeed, the first Tiger tank to be stopped in North Africa was stopped by a 6-pounder – but it needed better ammunition, because at more or less the same time as the gun went into service, the German tanks began using face-hardened armour. Capped-steel shot (APC) was issued in October 1942, followed by ballistically capped shot (APCBC), in January 1943; the latter improved performance to 88/1000/30 degrees. Finally, the first APDS shot to leave the muzzle at 4,050ft/sec (1,235m/sec) came just in time for D-Day in June 1944; this would

Firing a 2-pounder in the North African desert, 1941

57mm/6-pr Gun

The 6-pounder had a long record of service in the British Army and Royal Navy, since it was the first cased-charge gun to be adopted, in 1885. Its task was to shoot at torpedo-boats and other light, fast craft. Because of the Navy's involvement in the early tank programmes, the 6-pounder became the standard armament of the British tanks in 1916. The tank programmes of the 1920s departed from this and adopted a 3-pounder gun to fit inside the turret of the Vickers medium tank, but when the Royal Artillery began to contemplate something larger than the 2-pounder for anti-tank shooting, the 6-pounder was a logical choice. There was ample machinery for making barrels and ammunition, and a wealth of ballistic data available.

Instead of simply taking the well-tried coast-defence gun (which, by the 1930s, was virtually relegated to the practice role), a completely new design was drawn up in 1938, and in the following year a pilot gun was made and tested. Afterwards, the design was sealed and put away in the safe to await the day when it would be needed.

When that day came, in 1940, the outlook was bleak. The Army had lost 509 2-pounders and 98 25mm Hotchkiss guns in France, and anti-tank guns were vital for the defence of Britain when Hitler finally made up his mind to cross the Channel. If the 6-pounder went into production, it would be some months before the first guns reached the hands of troops, and the troops were trained to use them. On the other hand, if the existing production lines for the 2-pounder were kept running, guns would be despatched within days, to troops who were completely familiar with them, and they would be able to go straight into action. It is hardly surprising, therefore, that the 2-pounder was continued in production and the 6-pounder waited in the wings.

It was November 1941 before the first 6-pounder anti-tank guns came from the factories, but by May 1942 they were arriving at the rate of 1,500 guns per month. They first replaced the 2-pounder in Royal Artillery anti-tank batteries, then they were distributed to infantry battalions; their deployment was welcomed in the North African desert, where the Panzers of the Afrika Corps had been staved off only by deploying 25-pounders in anti-tank positions.

Although replaced in the RA by the 17-pounder, the 6-pounder continued to serve with the infantry until it became obsolete in July 1960.

The British 6-pounder anti-tank gun, which, with minor changes and no muzzle brake, was also the American 57mm gun

---

57mm/6-pr Gun continued

DATA (British 6-pr 7-cwt Mark 2 on Carriage Mk 1)

Calibre	2.244in (57mm)
Weight of gun and breech	768lb (348kg)
Total weight in action	2,521lb (1,143kg)
Barrel length	100.95in (2.564m)
Rifling	24 grooves, right-hand twist, one turn in 30 calibres
Recoil system and length	Hydro-spring, constant, 30in
Breech mechanism	Vertical sliding block, semi-automatic, percussion firing
Elevation	- 5 degrees to + 15 degrees
Traverse	45 degrees either side of zero
Projectiles and weights	HE 6.0lb (2.72kg); AP 6.25lb (2.83); APC 6.25lb (2.83); APCBC 7.0lb (3.17); APCR 3.97lb (1.80); APDS 3.25lb (1.61)
Muzzle velocities	HE 2,700ft/sec (823m/sec); AP 2,695 (821); APC, APCBC 2,775 (845); APCR 3,528 (1,075); APDS 4,050 (1,235)
Penetration	AP 74/1,000/30; APC 88/1,000/30; APCBC 95/1,000/30; APCR 100/1,000/30; APDS 146/1,000/30
Maximum range	5,500 yards (5,030m)

---

defeat 146/1000/30 degrees, in other words, defeating 5in of face-hardened armour, and actually going through 168mm or 6.6in of steel.

The 17-Pounder

Even before the 6-pounder went into production, the design of its successor was under way. On 21 November 1940, after briefly contemplating an 8-pounder (which would have the doubtful advantage of fitting into gun carriages and mountings designed for the 6-pounder), it was decided to go for a 3in (76mm) gun firing a 17lb (7.7kg) shot. The armaments design department was instructed to prepare a design and build a wooden mock-up. This was done by the spring of 1941 and, in spite of some misgivings over the size of the weapon, production was authorized and four pilot models were ordered in July. These were tested, and the 17-pounder gun was formally approved for service in May 1942. As well as being provided with an AP shot, it was also given a high-explosive shell, and

A 6-pounder gun mounted en portee *on the back of a 3-ton truck*

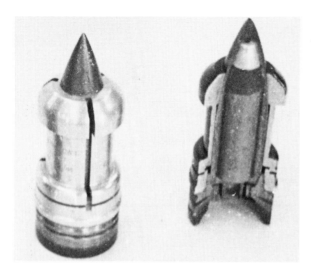

The APDS (armour piercing, discarding sabot) shot for the 6-pounder gun; left, as fired; right, cut open to show the tungsten carbide core and the construction of the sabot

with this it could reach a range of 10,000 yards, which gave it a useful field artillery back-up capability, though, in practice, this was rarely used.

With the AP shot, it could defeat 109/1000/30 degrees, and this was very soon increased by the provision of an APC shot to 118/1000/30 degrees. Following on the successful development of APDS for the 6-pounder, a design of APDS for the 17-pounder was approved in April 1944, and first supplies of this ammunition reached the front line in August 1944. This gave the ability to defeat 231/1000/30 degrees, which was enough to see off anything the enemy had, provided the gunner held his breath and let it get close enough.

The 32-Pounder

Throughout the war, an eye was kept on the development of tanks and, by late 1942, it was time to make some decisions about the next generation of anti-tank weapons. In October 1942, the General Staff asked for a new design, which would give at least a 25 per cent improvement on the performance of the 17-pounder. The ballistics experts studied their slide rules, and announced that the solution would be a 4.5in gun firing a 55lb (25kg) shot – or, in simpler terms, the current 4.5in AA gun mounted on a field carriage and given a suitable projectile.

No one will ever know what this monster might have looked like – the barrel alone would have weighed some 2.5 tons – since before it could be designed the Ordnance Board pointed out that, with the future APDS shot, the 17-pr could better the performance predicted for the 55-pr. In April 1943, the idea was dropped and a 30-pounder gun was proposed instead.

This was basically the existing 3.7in AA gun on an anti-tank mounting, with some modifications to the chamber and rifling, to provide for a large propelling charge and an APDS shot. Approval was given for a prototype in January 1944. It was predicted that a solid shot of 37lb (16.8kg) would give the optimum performance, so the new weapon became the '37-pounder EX1' in its towed form, and 'EX2' in self-propelled form. In June 1944, firing trials showed that the 37lb (16.8kg) shot was a failure and a 32lb (14.5kg) version more effective, so the gun was re-christened as the 32-pounder.

Two different carriages were designed; both were two-wheeled split-trail patterns with shields. One, by the armaments design department, used a conventional recoil system and a special muzzle brake, developing 75 per cent efficiency. The other, by a Mr Stevens, used a recoil system of his own design, which incorporated a means of pumping the gun back in its cradle for transport, and which

Ordnance, QF, 17-pr Gun Mark 1 on Carriage Mark 1

The 17-pounder was the result of a conference held on 7 May 1941 to discuss the future anti-tank gun. The first suggestion was for an 8-pounder, which would keep the overall size of the weapon the same as the 6-pounder, but would give a better performance. This was given short shrift, the general opinion being that a bigger gun was the only solution. As a result, a 3in 17-pounder was designed and by August 1941 a wooden mock-up had been made. There were some comments about the size of the equipment, but it was approved and, in view of the urgency, an immediate order was given for the manufacture of 500 guns, without waiting for pilot models. It was hoped that the first 200 would be ready by the end of 1942, for issue to corps anti-tank regiments.

The carriage, which had to withstand a formidable recoil force, gave some difficulties in design, and, in September 1942, intelligence having got wind of the imminent arrival of the German 'Tiger' tank in North Africa, a number of 17-pounder barrels were mounted on 25-pounder carriages and hurriedly shipped out. This was officially the '17-pr Gun Mk 1 on Carriage Mk 2', but it was more usually referred to by its code name 'Pheasant'. In the event, the first Tiger tank to be claimed by a British anti-tank gun fell to a 6-pounder.

The 17-pr was originally provided with a plain steel AP shot; shortly after that, it received a capped shot, and by June 1942 a design of discarding sabot shot was being explored. This was worked on throughout 1943, and eventually reached the hands of troops in August 1944, whereupon it became the supreme tank killer on the Allied side. It was later to be mounted in self-propelled equipments and in tanks. A slightly modified version, the Mark 3, with the breech converted to manual operation only, was issued to the Royal Navy and mounted in turrets on gun landing craft, for support during the initial landing of troops on hostile beaches.

DATA

Calibre	3.0in (76.2mm)
Weight of gun and breech	1,822lb (826kg)
Total weight in action	4,624lb (2,097kg)
Barrel length	180.35in (4.58m) with muzzle brake
Rifling	20 grooves, right hand, one turn in 30 calibres
Recoil system and length	Hydro-pneumatic, constant, 40in (1,016mm)
Breech mechanism	Vertical sliding block, semi-automatic, percussion firing
Elevation	- 6 degrees to + 16.5 degrees
Traverse	30 degrees either side of zero
Projectiles and weights	HE 15.7lb (7.12kg); AP 16.94 (7.68); APC 17.0 (7.71); APCBC 17.0 (7.71); APDS 7.63 (3.46)
Muzzle velocities	HE 2,875ft/sec (876m/sec); AP, APC, APCBC 2,900 (884); APDS 3,950 (1,203)
Penetration	AP 109/1,000/30; APC 118/1,000/30; APDS 231/1,000/30
Maximum range	10,000 yards (9,144m)

The 17-pounder gun; the white lines were not normal markings, but applied for test purposes

The breech end of the 17-pounder gun. The large tubular casing at the left side of the breech contains the powerful spring that closed the breech automatically as the cartridge was inserted. The metal fitting at the bottom right of the breech is the cam, which opened the breech as the gun ran out after recoiling

required a muzzle brake of only 40 per cent efficiency.

Work continued through 1945, but the war was over by the time the designs were ready, and it was obvious that the anti-tank gun had reached the end of its development line. Precise figures are not available, but the towed equipment must have weighed close to ten tons, and manhandling it in and out of concealed positions was totally impractical. In September 1945, the General Staff ruled that there was no longer any requirement for the weapon, and in the following month the Director of Artillery said, 'It is not being perpetuated in service and only limited trials will be carried out.' These were completed in 1946 (indeed, at Larkhill in 1946, I was told by one of the

The 17-pounder Mark 2 was a 17-pr gun mounted on the carriage of the 25-pounder, sent to North Africa to deal with the Tiger tank

trials squad that tests with infra-red night-sights had been part of the programme); the Stevens carriage gun went to the Royal Artillery Museum, while the other was scrapped.

The 25mm Hotchkiss and the 37mm Bofors

There were two more anti-tank guns in British service in the early part of the war. The first was the French 25mm Hotchkiss, which had been adopted as a stop-gap until sufficient 2-pounders were produced, and was officially issued to Territorial Army formations. The slow production of 2-pounders led to a few Regular units being equipped with them as well. Most were left behind in France in 1940, and those that remained in England lasted only as long as the stock of ammunition. Almost all had vanished by mid-1941.

The other equipment was the 37mm Bofors L/45, numbers of which had been bought by the Sudanese Army in the late 1930s. These were taken over and used by units of the British 8th Army in the Western Desert in 1941. Of conventional two-wheel, split-trail form, with small shields, they fired a 700g (25oz) AP shell at 800m/sec (2,625ft/sec), which, on a good day, could defeat 32/500/0 degrees. Most were worn out or lost in the course of the desert campaign. They were assimilated into British service as the 'Ordnance QF 37mm Mk 1 on Carriage 37mm Mk 1', and were formally declared obsolete as late as May 1947.

The Burney Gun

The second anti-tank diversion was the recoilless gun. This wartime development was entirely due to one man, Commander Sir Denistoun Burney. He had invented the 'Paravane' mine-sweeping device during the First World War, designed airships, developed and manufactured a streamlined motor car in the late 1920s, and in 1940 he began working on recoilless guns. He had no knowledge of German work in this area, and based his work on scientific principles, and on his knowledge of the Davis gun of the First World War.

The Davis gun was, put simply, a gun with a

Rear view of the 17-pr Mark 2. The only thing which indicates this is not a 25-pounder is the spring casing on the breech.

The 32-pounder anti-tank gun

Breech end of the 32-pounder gun. The piping around the recoil system is part of a hydraulic arrangement for pumping the gun back in its cradle for transport, to relieve the elevating gear from stress due to the long barrel. The bar behind the breech ring is a safety device to prevent the gun slipping back (this is an exhibit at the RA Museum, Woolwich)

Front view of the 32-pr gun at Woolwich; compare its size with the 5.5in medium gun alongside

chamber and a barrel at each end of it. A shell went in the front barrel, a cartridge in the chamber, and a weight of lead shot and grease equal to the weight of the shell went into the rear barrel. On firing the cartridge, shell and 'countershot' went down their respective barrels at the same velocity and each delivered the same recoil force. Since they were moving in opposite directions, the two forces cancelled each other out, and the gun did not move. The Royal Naval Air Service tried such a gun in 1918 as an anti-submarine weapon, but the war ended before much work had been done.

Following simple arithmetic, the recoilless gun becomes more practical. Instead of firing an equal weight out of two barrels, half the weight of countershot can be fired at twice the velocity; as long as the momentum (mass x velocity) is the same, recoil is cancelled out. Burney worked out that this can be carried to its ultimate extent by discharging a volume of propellant gas from the back of the gun at very high velocity. His final design used a cartridge case perforated with holes in its side; four-fifths of the gas generated by the explosion of the cartridge passed through these holes, and was directed through venturi jets (convergent-divergent nozzles, which accelerate the gases as they flow through them) at the rear of the gun. Because much of the gas is used in this way, the barrel of the gun can be quite thin and light, and the extra weight of a strong carriage and a recoil system are no longer necessary; the carriage just needs to be strong enough to support the weight of the gun.

Burney's master-stroke was to develop a special projectile, which he called the 'wall-buster'. Because of the low stresses on the shell, it could be made of thinner metal than a conventional shell; he then filled it with plastic explosive supported by a metal mesh, and put a fuze in the shell's base end. On striking the target, the light metal collapsed, and the plastic explosive in its mesh bag spread on to the face of the target like a sticky poultice. The base fuze then detonated it and drove a powerful shockwave into the target. This wave passed through the target mass until it reached the other

The 3.45in recoilless gun; because of its calibre it came to be called 'the 25-pounder shoulder gun'. It took a reasonably strong man to carry it, let alone fire it off the shoulder, but it could be done

side, and then bounced back, giving rise to what is called the 'pressure-bar effect'; in practical terms, it shakes loose a solid chunk of the target material and flings it off. If the target is a tank, a slab of steel weighing several pounds flies off on the inside of the armour at several hundred feet per second, and whirls round inside the tank, wrecking everything.

Two Burney guns were designed primarily as anti-tank weapons. One was 3.45in in calibre and could be fired off a man's shoulder or from a light tripod. The other was 3.7in in calibre, and carried on a light two-wheeled mounting. The 'Ordnance RCL 3.45in Mk 1' weighed 75lb (34kg), was 68.5in (1.74m) long, and fired an 11lb (5kg) wallbuster shell to 1,000 yards. No penetration figures were ever made public, but it is fairly certain that it could

The 3.7in recoilless gun showed a great deal of promise as an anti-tank weapon, but it came too late

knock a 10lb (4.5kg) slab off the back of 6in (150mm) of armour plate at any range it could hit.

The 3.7 was a larger weapon, weighing 222lb (100kg); it was 112in (2.84m) long and fired a 22.2lb (10kg) wallbuster to 2,000 yards; it is estimated that this could have dealt successfully with armour up to 10in (254mm) thick.

Both weapons were overtaken by events, with the war ending before they could be put into production. Both were produced in limited numbers in 1945–46 and were used for extensive user trials,

but they were then withdrawn and scrapped. After this time, development of recoilless guns took a different direction under different management.

THE USA

The 37mm Guns

In 1918, the American Army acquired some 3,200 37mm 'Trench Guns' from the French. This was a

Breech end of the 3.7in RCL gun, showing the six jets surrounding the breech

miniature version of the 75mm M1897, using the same sort of Nordenfelt screw breech, but only 31in long, and firing a 1.25lb (0.5kg) shell to a maximum range of 4,900 yards (4,500m). It may have served some purpose as a trench-warfare weapon, but as a field weapon it was quite useless. Nevertheless, the Army spent the 1920s trying to improve it and eventually produced the '37mm Gun M2' in 1929. However, since this gun only fired a solid shot in the anti-tank role, and because the new carriage was overweight, it was eventually thrown out. By 1933, the US Army had no anti-tank capability at all, apart from the .50 Browning machine gun.

Work on a new gun began in 1937 with the purchase of two 37mm Rheinmetall PaK36 guns from Germany. After studying these, the designers produced three pilot models: the T7, using a semi-automatic horizontal sliding block breech; the T8, using a Nordenfelt screw breech; and the T10, with a hand-operated vertical sliding block breech. After comparative tests, the T10 was selected, and standardized as the 37mm Gun M3 in October 1938.

The design – a two-wheeled split-trail carriage with shield and hydro-spring recoil system – was quite conventional. It had 30 degrees of traverse on either side and weighed only 912lb (414kg) in action. It fired a 1.92lb (870-g) AP shell to a maximum range of 12,850 yards (11,790m), and it could defeat 36mm of armour at 500 yards (460m) at normal. An APC shot was later produced, which increased performance to 61/500/0 degrees.

(Note: unfortunately, during the war years, AP performance was not measured at exactly the same angle of impact in all countries, so direct comparison between different weapons is not always possible.)

A later improvement to the 37mm Gun M3 was the adoption of a five-port muzzle brake to cut down the recoil force and, possibly, admit of a more powerful charge. Gun barrels had the requisite thread cut on their muzzles, advancing them to the M3A1 model. Although authorized in 1941, the brake was never issued, probably because the Americans had realized by then that souping up the

37mm was pointless. The gun still had a role to play against light armour, and it was certainly capable of holding its own against the Japanese tanks encountered in the Pacific campaign, and production continued until over 18,000 had been made. However, the soldiers had studied the reports from Poland in 1939 and France in 1940 and knew that, if they ever came up against the Germans, they would need something better than a 37mm gun.

The 57mm Gun M1

Clearly, the Americans had the services of some good gun designers, but by late 1940 they were all hard at work putting the finishing touches to designs that had been roughed out in the pauper years, and were now about to come to life. The quickest solution to the anti-tank gun problem was to find one which appeared to be effective, and copy it. The best available was the British 6-pounder, so in February 1941 the Ordnance Committee authorized the preparation of production drawings based on the British design. They took a set of production drawings, supplied from Britain, and changed all the tolerances, threads, bolt sizes and gear sizes to American standards, as well as making sundry minor modifications, such as adjusting the sight brackets to take American telescopes, and the wheels to take American tyres. The one significant difference was that the American gun had a barrel 16in (406mm) longer than the British gun. Once these modifications had been made, the design was standardized as the 57mm Gun M1, on 15 May 1941.

(In fact, the British gun should have been 16in longer, but the lack of gun lathes of the necessary length had caused the design to be modified. The Americans had no such shortage of machine tools. The British gun was duly lengthened in later marks, as the lathes became available. It made a difference of just over 100ft/sec in muzzle velocity.)

The performance of the 57mm Gun M1 was much the same as that of the 6-pounder Mark 1, the significant difference being that the Americans preferred the piercing shell as their standard

The American 57mm RCL gun in action in the Pacific. Note the characteristic perforated cartridge case, and the pre-grooved driving band. The jets in this weapon were simply radial slots surrounding the chamber opening and venting through slots in the breech block

projectile. A plain steel shot (the M79) was provided, but the standard item was the 'Projectile APC M86' a capped shell weighing 7.27lb (3.3kg) and carrying a charge of 1.2oz of Explosive D, and a base fuze M72. This could defeat 79mm of face-hardened armour at 1,000 yards at 20 degrees.

That was as far as it went; there was no further development of ammunition for the 57mm gun, neither tungsten-cored shot, nor APDS. The 57mm continued to serve throughout the war, even though towards the end it was struggling to deal with the heavier German armour. Some effort was wasted on various self-propelled exercises, but generally no development work was done on the gun once it was

The other US recoilless gun to get into service was this 75mm weapon. Both guns fired HEAT projectiles against tanks and, as shown here, high-explosive shells against other targets

The American 37mm anti-tank gun was broadly copied from the German Rheinmetall PaK 36

The arrival of the Jeep in 1941 led to many pictures such as this, embodying the spirit of the tank-destroyer philosophy

A 37mm gun in North Africa, 1942, looking for customers

American Airborne troops on D-Day, with their glider-landed 57mm gun and jeep

in service. This might have been due to the belief that the 57mm would be replaced by a better gun fairly soon.

The 3in M5

In September 1940, the Army demanded an anti-tank gun capable of stopping any tank in the world. The ordnance department decided that the easiest way to deal with this problem was to reach into the spare parts bin and see what they could put together. This may sound dismissive, but in fact it produced what could have been a world-beater. Their formula was to take the barrel of a 3in anti-aircraft gun and fit it on to the carriage of the standard 105mm howitzer M2, adding the 105's breech mechanism for good measure. All they now had to do was provide this 3in M5 gun with some ammunition and

Anti-tank guns can be useful for other tasks; an American 57mm attacking a Japanese pillbox in the Philippines, May 1945

the job was done. At which point, plans went awry.

The first setback came from Tank Destroyer Command, who were loud in their preference for self-propelled anti-tank weapons. A new design, the Gun Motor Carriage M5, was under development, and the TD Command was able to hold up production of the 3in towed gun until the SP model had been tested, in case the SP proved to be a better equipment. The GMC M5 worked, but was hopelessly impractical, so the towed gun project was reluctantly revived, and the gun was put into production.

The next discovery was that the ammunition was poor. Scaling up from the 57mm designs appeared not to work, and scaling down from heavier designs used in coast artillery was equally ineffectual. Particularly, the base fuzes either detonated the shell too soon, before it had gone through the plate, or failed to detonate it at all. Penetration figures never reached those that were theoretically possible, and confidence in the gun began to evaporate. If the delay imposed by the TD Command had been used to sort out the ammunition problems, the gun might have got off to a better start.

In the end, the problems were solved, and the 3in M5 was widely used in the European theatre. Firing its standard 15lb (6.8kg) AP shell, it could defeat 100/1000/0 degrees, which was good, but not as good as it ought to have been. Moreover, as with the 57mm, no further development work ever took place.

The 76mm T3, T4, T5

Work on the M5 seems to have been abandoned partly because all available energy and brain-power was being employed on two guns, which, it was hoped, would be available as both towed and SP anti-tank guns, and also as tank guns. Of these options, the tank gun got all the attention.

The 76mm gun began as a tank gun, with a better performance than the standard 75mm gun, but of a size which would fit into a turret, which the 3in M5 gun could not. Its advancement as a tank gun went

ahead at full speed, and it was also adopted as a self-propelled anti-tank gun, but, although it was proposed as a towed gun as early as June 1943, progress was slow. Three designs were put forward: the T4 was a scaled-up 57mm carriage; the T5 was an unusual design, in which the shield formed part of the carriage structure (rather than being a sheet of metal hung on as an afterthought) and had the trail legs hinged directly to it; and the T3 was basically a 3in M5 carriage with the new gun fitted into it. All of these designs had various defects, and the war ended without a 76mm towed gun being approved.

The 90mm T5, T8, T9

The 90mm gun was a conversion of the 90mm anti-aircraft gun and the project was launched early in 1943. By the end of the year, two experimental equipments had been built. The T5 was a conventional split-trail design, but the carriage weighed almost four tons before the gun was on it, and the designers were sent back to get the weight down. The T9 carriage was similar to the 76mm T5, using the shield as a structural member, and hanging the trail legs from the top corners. In action, the gun rested on a central pedestal, the wheels being lifted from the ground. For towing, the legs folded forward and locked to the barrel. Work on this began in January 1944, but was halted in July, when the design staff were wanted for other tasks. It was re-started in September 1944, but development was still in progress when the war ended.

The T5 carriage was reduced in weight but other defects appeared and the project was shelved in favour of the T9. It was revived in August 1944 but, as with the T9, it was not completed when the war ended. It was, eventually, produced in limited numbers in 1946–47, but it was never standardized.

The final venture, parallel with the British 32-pounder, was the 105mm Gun T8. This, too, began as a tank gun, the 105mm T5 of 48 calibres length. In mid-1944, it was lengthened to 65 calibres, to reach the magic 3,000ft/sec velocity figure, and

3in Gun M5 on Carriage M1, M1A1 or M6

The 3in gun M5, in the firing position

The US Army, having studied reports on the Polish and French campaigns, and with an eye to the probable future development of German tanks, realized quite rapidly that their 37mm anti-tank gun was not going to remain an effective weapon for very long. In 1941, therefore, they demanded a powerful gun capable of dealing with any tank then known, and with sufficient reserve of power to cope with anything likely to appear in the future. To speed up development, they ransacked the stores cupboard to see what could be adapted, and took the 3in AA gun M3 as the ordnance, fitting it with the breech mechanism of the 105mm howitzer. The carriage and recoil systems were also those of the 105mm howitzer, allowing the use of current production lines; with a little cutting and sawing here and there, the whole thing went together quite nicely, producing a very potent gun.

Unfortunately, the development of ammunition for the gun did not go so smoothly; a serviceable solid shot was produced, and a high-explosive shell, but the US Army was committed to the AP shell, and the development of a base fuze for this shell gave considerable trouble. While this was being worked on, the Army Ground Forces decided that a self-propelled equipment was more important, and they put the 3in towed gun programme on hold in order to test a design of SP gun. This, the Gun Motor Carriage T1, was the 3in AA gun with an all-enveloping shield mounted on a turntable placed on the back end of a large agricultural tractor, the Cletrac MG-2. There were two seats for the gun-layers, no room for the rest of the gun detachment, and no room for any ammunition. It is impossible to imagine now what possessed the Army Ground Forces Board ever to consider this device as a practical weapon, but it was eventually standardized as the GMC 3inch M5. No sooner was it standardized than it was quietly forgotten, and the 3in towed gun programme was revived, standardized as the M1 gun on carriage M1, and put into production.

The ammunition problems were eventually overcome and the 3in became a useful weapon; the US 1st and 3rd Armies in Europe deployed 301 guns between them and fired off 399,834 rounds between D-Day and the end of the war in Europe. The real trouble with the 3in gun was a distinct lack of enthusiasm in getting it into service and 'selling it' to the troops; instead of improving the ammunition by producing APCR or APDS shot, the development agencies preferred to abandon the 3in and concentrate their efforts on a new 76mm design, which, in the event, never got anywhere near service during the war.

3in Gun M5 on Carriage M1, M1A1 or M6 continued

DATA

Calibre	3.00in (76.2mm)
Weight of gun and breech	1,990lb (903kg)
Total weight in action	4,875lb (2,211kg)
Barrel length	158.4 in (4.023m)
Rifling	28 grooves, right-hand twist, one turn in 25 calibres
Recoil system and length	Hydro-pneumatic, constant, 42in (1,067mm)
Breech mechanism	Horizontal sliding block, manual, percussion firing
Elevation	- 5 degrees to + 30 degrees
Traverse	22.5 degrees either side of zero
Projectiles and weights	HE 12.87lb (5.84kg); AP Shot 15lb (6.8kg); APC/HE 15.43lb (7.0kg)
Muzzle velocities	HE, APC/HE 2,800ft/sec (853m/sec); AP 2,600ft/sec (792m/sec)
Penetration	APC/HE 102mm/1,000 yards/0 degrees
Maximum range	16,100 yards (14,720m)

proposals for putting it on to a wheeled carriage appeared. Development continued throughout 1945, the war ended, and the Army could see no requirement for it, but the ordnance department pushed on with two pilot models. These were tested in February 1946, the designers congratulated themselves, and then the project was closed down. It fired a 39lb (17.7kg) AP shell at 3,100ft/sec (945m/sec) to a maximum range of 27,000 yards (24,690m), and the penetration was claimed as 210/1000/0 degrees. However, it weighed eight tons, and, like the 32-pounder, was simply too cumbersome to be an effective field weapon.

RUSSIA

Russia, the darkest of dark horses in 1939, had been working at anti-tank gun designs since the middle 1920s, and had a varied collection. They had copied a German 37mm design in 1930, but the most they could wring out of it was 38/350/30 degrees; in 1930, the Russians had probably the best tanks in the world, so they were in a good position to appreciate that such a performance was not good enough. They upped the calibre to 45mm in 1932, to obtain 60mm at 500m at normal, and thereafter modified the design without improving the ballistic

An interesting comparison between the 37mm and 3in anti-tank guns

A 3in gun of the 94th Division, 3rd US Army, firing across the river Rhine near Krefeld, April 1945

performance, but making the equipment more robust and reliable. Eventually, the 45mm M1937 became their standard, but large numbers of the 1932 model remained in service, and it is not easy to distinguish between them. Both were simple two-wheeled split-trail carriages, more or less scaled up from the 37mm Rheinmetall design, and with tubular trail legs and wire-spoked wheels with pneumatic tyres. Both weighed 450kg (992lb) in the firing position, rather more when rigged for horse draught.

The 57mm

By 1940, it was clear that the 45mm gun was reaching the end of its useful life (although it was kept in service throughout the war), and a fresh design of 57mm gun was drawn up. This was no coincidence, since this had been a standard naval calibre since the Tsar's days, when six-pounder guns had been acquired from Armstrong's of Britain; six-pounders had also been acquired with various early British tanks that had found their way

The 90mm T13 gun on Carriage T9, an interesting prototype which got no further. The trail legs folded forward to lie alongside the barrel for towing

The 105mm Gun T8 on Carriage T19 was the American equivalent of the British 32-pounder – a superlative tank killer but totally impractical in the field (Photograph courtesy of Richard Hunnicutt)

The 105mm Gun T9 in the travelling position; the top carriage and gun have been revolved to bring the barrel over the trails

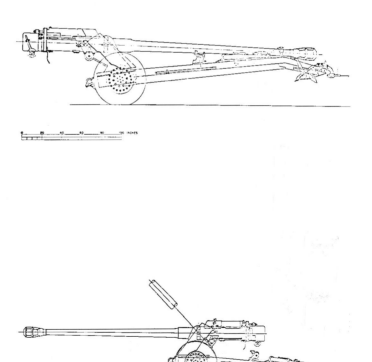

The 105mm Gun T9 in the firing position

The French 47mm M1937 gun; a luxury specification, but there were not enough of them

into Russian hands. The gun they produced was the best of its class anywhere; instead of the 50-calibre barrel adopted by Britain and the USA, the Russians went for a 73-calibre long barrel, which launched a 3.14kg (6.9lb) AP shot at 990m/sec (3,250ft/sec) to defeat 86/500/30 degrees. They were able to improve this in 1943 by introducing a tungsten-cored shot weighing 1.76kg (3.88lb), which left the muzzle at 1,270m/sec (4,160ft/sec) to defeat 100/500/30 degrees.

APCR

Fourteen millimetres may not seem much of a gain in performance for a 280m/sec gain in velocity; this is related to one of the effects of the w/d3 problem. The shot used by the Russians was copied from a German design called 'Arrowhead' shot, from its shape. The body of the shot was steel and light alloy, and tapered very sharply from the point to the shoulder. The diameter was severely reduced all the way back to the driving band area, where it abruptly

British troops manning a French 25mm Hotchkiss gun in 1940

The Soviet 45mm M1943

57mm Gun M1943 (ZIS-2)

The Soviet 57mm M1943, a far more powerful 57mm than that of the British and US forces

The 57mm calibre was familiar to the Soviets, since it had been used as a naval and coast-defence gun since before the turn of the century. When the Army decided to move up in calibre from its 45mm, this was an obvious choice. The first model was the M1941, which used a 70-calibre barrel mounted on a carriage adapted from that of the 76mm M1941 field gun. This used girder-section trail legs, which, apparently, did not have sufficient strength to withstand active service conditions. As a result, only a relatively small number entered service before this defect appeared, and the design was quickly changed to use tubular steel trail legs for both weapons. The anti-tank gun then became the M1943. It used the same barrel and breech, and the ballistic performance was the same; the change of trail legs and a small modification to the shield increased the weight by 25kg, but this was of little consequence.

The M1943 was an excellent weapon, probably the best of its calibre, and it remained in service throughout the war, even though heavier weapons came along. It even remained in service after the war, although not with Soviet forces, who relegated it to the reserve. It was adopted by several Warsaw Pact armies, and was in first-line service with some of them until the mid-1970s. The gun was also adapted to a lightweight self-propelled mounting used by Soviet airborne forces in the 1950s to 1970s.

57mm Gun M1943 (ZIS-2) continued

DATA

Calibre	57mm (2.244in)
Weight of gun and breech	n/a
Total weight in action	1,150kg (2,535lb)
Barrel length	3.945m (155.33in)
Rifling	24 grooves, right-hand, one turn in 30 calibres
Recoil system and length	Hydro-pneumatic, constant, 1.00m (39.34in)
Breech mechanism	Vertical sliding block, semi-automatic, percussion firing
Elevation	- 5 degrees to + 25 degrees
Traverse	28 degrees either side of zero
Projectiles and weights	HE 3.75kg (8.27lb); AP/HE 3.14 (6.92); AP/I 3.14 (6.92); HVAP 1/76 (3.88)
Muzzle velocities	HE 700m/sec (2,295ft/sec); AP/I, AP/HE 990 (3,250); HVAP 1185 (3,888)
Penetration	AP/HE 86/500/30; HVAP 100/500/30 and 102/1000/0
Maximum range	8,400m (9,185 yards)

came out to full calibre once more. Seen in silhouette, it looked rather like an arrowhead. Inside this was a core of tungsten carbide.

However, while the ratio of weight to diameter was favourable in the bore, and allowed the shot to get up to a fantastic velocity (for 1943), it remained the same after leaving the muzzle and was thus unfavourable for free flight, being too light to

sustain its velocity for long distances. At 200m, it was vastly superior to steel shot; at 500m, slightly superior, and at 1,000m, less effective. All the combatants tried this type of APCR ('armour-piercing, composite, rigid') shot, but the British abandoned it almost as soon as they adopted it; only the 6-pounder was ever given an APCR shot and it was soon ousted by the APDS.

The 76.2mm Divisional Gun M1936 was a useful anti-tank gun as well as being a field artillery weapon. Those captured by the Germans in 1941 were rapidly given muzzle brakes and better ammunition, and taken into German use as anti-tank guns. This one was captured by British forces in North Africa in late 1942

When the Germans invaded Russia in 1941 and the Panzers rampaged all over the steppes, the anti-tank gun became a vital weapon and the 57mm production was stepped up. A longer-barrelled version of the 45mm, the M1942, also appeared, which gave a slight gain in performance, and a second version of the 57mm gun, the M1943, appeared, differing only in having tubular trail legs and a somewhat simplified carriage to allow for quicker production.

Anti-Tank Ammunition for Field and Medium Guns

After that, the Russians did not make a 'pure' anti-tank gun for some time; instead, they took a remarkable policy decision. Any gun that had a tank within range and could engage it was, automatically, an anti-tank gun. Instead of developing anti-tank guns, anti-tank ammunition was developed for all the field and medium guns. Those that could generate sufficient velocity were given AP shot or Arrowhead tungsten-cored shot; those that fired at lower velocities were given shaped-charge shells. The 76mm M1942 field gun had a 3kg (6.6lb) arrowhead shot, which could defeat 92/500/0 degrees, as well as a steel AP shell that could defeat 69/500/0 degrees; the 85mm Divisional Gun D-44 had an arrowhead capable of 91/500/30 degrees. The 122mm field howitzer M1938 had a shaped-charge shell that would defeat 100mm of armour at 0 degrees at any range, while the 152mm gun-howitzer M37 had an AP shell capable of 125/1000/0 degrees. With this, the Russians broke the back of the Panzers.

By late 1943, this policy was less relevant, because the Germans were now fielding tanks with heavier armour, and a new anti-tank gun was needed. It appeared as the 100mm Model 1944, a conventional type of gun with a 54-calibre barrel, and three types of projectile: a 15.6kg (35lb) AP shell capable of 153/500/30 degrees, a 15.6kg (35lb) AP shot giving 186/500/30 degrees, and a 9.4kg (20.7lb) arrowhead shot giving 185/1000/0 degrees. With that, the Russian armoury was adequate for the remainder of the war.

6 Coast-Defence and Railway Artillery

BACKGROUND

Naval Strategy and Superiority

Coast-defence artillery and railway artillery come under the same heading for two reasons. First, as far as the Allies were concerned, neither saw a great deal of active service, and second, because the Allies frequently pressed railway guns into service as coast-defence weapons. Both facts were as a result of major strategy: in the Western hemisphere, the Allies had naval superiority, and coast defence was rarely called upon to defend against a naval threat; in the Eastern hemisphere, the immediate post-Pearl Harbor period of Japanese naval superiority in the Pacific Ocean called for a sudden strengthening of coast defences on the west coast of the USA, which could most easily be achieved by wheeling in railway guns.

It is important to distinguish coast-defence artillery 'proper' from hurried emplacement of guns, such as that which took place in Britain in the late summer of 1940. Coast artillery 'proper' means guns sited in peacetime in carefully built emplacements, to protect naval bases and strategic ports, linked together by a complex system of command and control with range-finding and observation facilities, searchlights and, in the latter part of the war, radar, and thus equipped to deal energetically and efficiently with a variety of naval threats.

Emergency Batteries

'Emergency batteries' appeared overnight in 1940 around the coast of Britain (and other places), and, mostly, disappeared as rapidly in 1944–45. They were simply equipped to deal with landing craft attempting to dump troops on the shore. They could have done useful work in this role, but they had little or no hope of taking on any sort of warship at any practical range, having neither the power nor the technical back-up in range-finding, fire control and observation. (On one or two occasions, an emergency battery filled an unsuspected gap in the 'proper' defences, and was therefore better armed and incorporated into the fortress system, but this did not happen often.)

The story of the emergency batteries in Britain cannot be fully explored here; there are four lists of emergency batteries, all of which contradict each other in the matter of locations and armament. The simple fact is that in the late summer of 1940 the principal task was to get guns emplaced, and the book-keeping and paperwork never really caught up. Gun ledgers recording the issue of guns disagree with records of guns actually mounted in given locations, and the locations quoted by some lists are, to say the least, peculiar. One example is Preston, Lancashire, apparently allocated two 4in QF guns, to the 'Officer Commanding RA, Preston' in 1940, but a most unlikely site for coast-defence guns. Where they went to is still a mystery. It could be the battery at Lytham St Annes, a few miles away, except that its guns are recorded as being BLs. It may be that the clerk making the lists did not know the difference between QF and BL, or perhaps he thought that 'BL' was part of the description of every gun? We shall never know. This sort of inconsistency sums up the problems

*Typical of the many emergency
batteries installed around the
British coastline in 1940 is this
naval 4in gun on a timber and
concrete platform, in the beach at
Blundellsands, Lancashire. It was
manned by the 385th Field Defence
Battery*

with emergency batteries, a ripe field for deep research.

Statistics

Although coast defence may not have had an active war, it was certainly prepared for almost any eventuality. A list prepared in June 1945, showing every British coast-defence gun installed throughout the world, produces some quite remarkable information. The total of 'proper' coast-defence batteries then armed was 352, which included forty in enemy hands (in Hong Kong, Singapore, Penang and Rangoon). The total of all coast-defence batteries, including emergency batteries in Britain and other countries throughout the Empire, and batteries installed in or taken over in captured territory, reached 710. Artillery ranged from two 6in BL guns at Hvalfjordur in Iceland to two 4in QFs in South Georgia; from three 9.2in BL guns in Albert Head Battery, Esquimault, British Columbia, to five 6in guns on the island of Fiji. One interesting statistic is the presence of two 6in, one 4in, two 12-pr and two 3-pr guns on the Falkland Islands.

Railway Artillery

The British railway artillery that had survived the First World War – which was not much – spent the Second World War parked on convenient sidings, from which it could bombard likely invasion

*A 12in gun on disappearing
mounting of Battery Crockett, Fort
Mills, Corregidor, after its recapture
from the Japanese in 1945*

beaches. Three guns were hastily assembled for the purpose of bombarding the German gun batteries on the French coast, although this may have been more of a public relations gesture than intended to do any real damage. There was a move to assemble a Super-Heavy Railway Regiment, and send it to France in the wake of the D-Day invasion, but, given the damage that the Tactical Air Forces had done to the French railway system, and the damage they could do to more or less anything else towards which they were pointed, wiser counsel prevailed and the idea was abandoned before it got very far. By early 1945, all the railway guns had been trundled away, to be scrapped as soon as the war was over. Not one remains.

American Coast and Railway Defence

American had a less far-flung domain than Britain in 1939, but it protected what it had with some of the most intensive coast artillery installations ever built. The Defenses of Manila and Subic Bay in the Philippines, for example, totalled five forts with thirty-four batteries mounting eighty-five guns, of calibres from 3 to 14in; the Panama Canal had six forts holding twenty-three batteries and fifty-nine guns from 6 to 16in calibre. Hawaii, and particularly Pearl Harbor, was also well protected, and the coasts of the USA, from Canada to the Mexican border, were ringed with ordnance. Moreover, the US Army was the beneficiary of the Washington Conference on Naval Limitation, which caused the US Navy to abandon a proposed programme of battleship-building and donate its 16in guns earmarked for that purpose to the Army for coast defence. During the 1930s, a handful of these had been emplaced, but the coming of war provided money to construct emplacements, particularly on the Pacific Coast, for several more.

American coast guns probably also fired more shots in anger than those of any other nation, since the guns of Manila Bay, particularly those of Fort Mills, Corregidor and Fort Drum, the 'Concrete Battleship', were heavily engaged during the operations in the Bataan Peninsula and the subsequent siege of Corregidor.

American railway artillery, like the British, consisted almost entirely of First World War designs, which had been retained in mothballs. The only exceptions were four 14in guns built in the 1920s, and a number of 8in guns built in 1940–41. Irrespective of age or calibre, they all ended up as coast-defence weapons, generally being integrated into the existing coast-defence command system, since they had been designed with this application in mind. A number were loaned to Canada in 1940 to protect the approaches to Esquimault harbour in British Columbia until British 9.2in guns could be emplaced, and various other improvements made to the defences there. After 1945, all guns were withdrawn, declared obsolete and scrapped. One solitary 8in gun and mounting, stripped from its railway car, remains in a park in Tampa, Florida; the only other US railway gun remaining is a 1918 model 14in of the US Navy, preserved in the Naval Museum in Washington DC.

Russia

The Russians seem to have directed their energies towards armoured trains rather than heavy artillery, and this certainly made sense. Russia consisted of vast areas to be patrolled, a limited railway network, which could never be guaranteed to go where it was needed, and had a railway gauge different from that of any of its neighbours. Armoured trains for protecting the territory and its lines of communication were far more useful than heavy guns, which were restricted to a handful of lines, and which could not move across the borders. Russia did make a handful of railway guns, however, one of which is particularly interesting, and did use them to some degree during the war.

Unfortunately, histories of Soviet artillery completely ignore the railway gun, possibly because general artillery was an Army affair, but the railway guns were a Navy responsibility, as an addition to the coast defences. Coast artillery is another area of mystery. The Russians undoubtedly had coast guns and howitzers, but no details have ever been made public and, apart from some reputed minor activity in the Crimea and the Baltic approaches to Leningrad, it seems unlikely that any of it saw much action. Coast artillery was also a naval affair, and there seems not to be any published history or description of it at all. In view of this, rather than relying on speculation, this book will leave Russian coast defence artillery out of the story.

BRITISH COAST DEFENCE

Britain had tidied up its coast-defence equipment inventory in the wake of the First World War, casting out obsolete and non-standard guns and carriages, and retaining only four calibres: the 3in 12-pounder, the 4.7in, the 6in and the 9.2in. Within these calibres there was a variety of models, but there was standardization of ammunition within each calibre, and the roles of the various calibres were specifically defined. The 12-pr and 4.7 could deal with torpedo-boats, the 6in with boom-smashers and raiding warships, and the 9.2 was the counter-bombardment gun for subduing major warships at long range.

In the mid-1920s, however, the question of arming the new naval base at Singapore arose, and it seemed that, Washington Conference or not, the Japanese were intent upon having really big battleships. Singapore also had large areas of water in which high-speed torpedo-boats could play havoc, and something with a much better rate of fire than the 12-pounder was desirable. The naval 15in gun was selected as the major armament capable of taking on anything afloat; this meant that some superior range and position-finding equipment had to be developed, to take advantage of the available range. For the torpedo-boats, a new two-barrelled 6-pounder appeared to offer a suitable answer.

The 12-Pounder

Of the older guns, the 12-pounder QF gun dated from 1894, and was invariably mounted on a simple pedestal with a shield. It fired a separate-loading round, in which the shell was rammed first and followed up by the brass cartridge case. It had an unusual design feature; when introduced it was for naval defence against torpedo-boats, and the sailors in those days still worked in bare feet. A 12-pr cartridge case, forcefully ejected and falling to the

A 12-pounder 12-cwt QF coast gun in its proper emplacement, serving as a beach-defence gun in 1940

165

Coast-Defence and Railway Artillery

To provide instant coast defence in captured ports, the 6in Mark 7 coast gun was mounted on this 'Arrol-Withers Platform', and could be brought into position on a tank transporter

deck, could do serious injury; the breech was given an extractor, which loosened the cartridge case in the chamber, but not an ejector. Instead, the primer protruded from the base of the case (there was a recess in the front face of the breech-block to accommodate it), and had a raised rim. One of the gun detachment held an iron claw, with which he gripped the primer rim as the breech was opened and jerked out the cartridge case, flinging it in a safe direction as the next round was being loaded.

For convenience, the land-service guns used the same construction and ammunition, even though the soldiers wore stout boots. In the early 1930s, with the Navy decently shod, it was decided that there was no point in perpetuating this system, and guns began to be fitted with ejectors. Nevertheless, a large number of the old pattern remained in service, and hand ejection was still a regular practice.

The 12-pounder fired a 12.5lb (5.7kg) shell at 2,257ft/sec to reach a maximum range of 10,100 yards (9,265m). This may not seem much, but bearing in mind its short-range role and the fact that it was a direct-fire eye-shooting gun, this was more than adequate.

The 4.7in QF Gun

The 4.7in QF gun was even older than the 12-pounder, having first appeared as a naval gun in

1887. Over the years there had been a bewildering variety of different marks and models, but by 1939 most had been cleared away, and the usual model was a 40- or 45-calibre gun, mounted on a low-set pedestal with a shield, and firing a useful 45lb (20.5kg) shell. Like the 12-pounder, it was a separate-loading round of ammunition, and used the protruding primer and the hand ejection system. With a muzzle velocity of 2,150 or 2,350ft/sec, it could reach a range of 13,000 (11,925m) or 16,500 yards (15,140m), depending upon which mark of gun was being used; again, its performance was satisfactory for its particular role.

The 6in Mark VII and the Mark 24

The 6in BL gun first appeared in 1882, but the Mark VII gun on Mounting, Central Picot Mark II, the near-universal coast-defence medium gun, dated from 1898. It was a pedestal mounting in a concrete pit, the gun protected by a shield. It could be directed by a fire-control room, using indicator dials in the gun pit and operated by hand controls in the pit, beneath the gun's working platform. Alternatively, it could be directly laid by two gun-layers on the platform using the 'autosight', a form of telescope sight which, when laid on the bow-wave of the target, automatically elevated the gun to the correct range. It used separate-loading bag charge ammunition, firing a 100lb (45kg) shell at

166

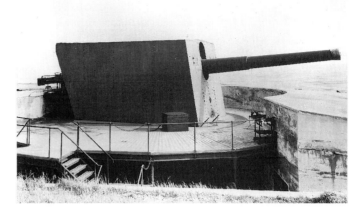

The 9.2in gun Mark 10 on Mounting Mark 7, the standard British coast-defence counter-bombardment gun

2,558ft/sec to reach 19,700 yards (18,075m) range with the most modern ammunition. It could defeat its own calibre of cemented (face-hardened) armour at 3,000 yards range.

The principal defect of the Mark II mounting was the maximum elevation of 20 degrees, which limited the maximum range. However, until the late 1920s there was no great demand to improve this, because of the range and position-finding systems then in use. There was no particular point in having a gun that could fire further than the target could be plotted. When improved systems were developed in the 1920s, the demand for more range grew, and it was answered by the Mark 24 gun on Mounting Mark 5 or Mark 6.

The Mark 24 had essentially the same barrel as the Mark VII gun, but a modern and more efficient breech mechanism. The Mounting Mark 5 was essentially the Central Pivot Mark II, but with an all-enclosing gun-house instead of a shield, and with the ability to elevate the gun to 45 degrees. This gave the gun a maximum range of 24,500 yards (22,475m). (The Mark 6 mounting differed in some design details only.)

The 9.2in BL Gun Mark X

The standard heavy or 'counter-bombardment' gun was the 9.2in BL Gun Mark X on Mounting,

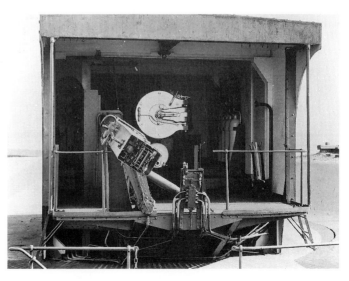

Rear view of the Mark 7 9.2in mounting, showing the rammer swung to the left, clear of the breech, to permit the gun to recoil

Barbette Mark V. This was another venerable weapon, which had appeared in coast defences in the late 1880s, and was to continue (as did all the other guns) until 1956. There were, through the years, a wide range of marks of guns and mountings, but by 1939 the museum pieces had been culled, and the Mark X on Mounting V had become the universal standard; a few had been improved to the Mounting Mark VI, which allowed 30 degrees of elevation instead of the 15 degrees of the Mark V, and a handful to Mark VII standard, which gave 35 degrees of elevation. The maximum range varied accordingly; a Mark V mounting allowed 21,000 yards (19,265m), a Mark VI, 29,500 yards (27,065m), and a Mark VII, 36,700 yards (33,670m), all firing the standard 380lb (172.75kg) AP shell, propelled at 2,700ft/sec by a 125lb (57kg) charge of Cordite.

The Mountings

Barbette Mountings

The barbette mountings were all similar. A concrete pit 35ft in diameter and 11ft deep held a massive cast-steel pedestal in its centre, on top of which the gun-mounting revolved on a roller race, driven either by hand (Marks V and VI) or by hydraulic power (Mark VII). The pedestal area was covered by a massive steel roof called the 'shell-pit shield', which acted as a working platform for part of the gun detachment – the gun-layers, the gun commander (or 'Number One'), the breech operator, and the loading numbers.

Beneath the shield, on the floor of the pit, were the rest of the detachment, handling the ammunition. This arrived at a hatch in the pit wall by lift from the underground magazine, shells on one side of the pit, cartridges on the other. (A cardinal rule in coast artillery was that shell and cartridge never met until they were inside the gun.) The shell was raised by a hydraulic lift and clipped to a trolley running on rails beneath the shell-pit shield. It was trundled round by one of the handlers until it was beneath the breech of the gun. When the Number One ordered 'Load!', he pulled a lever to actuate a hydraulic ram, which lifted the shell from its trolley, pushed it through a trap-door in the shield, and aligned it with the open breech. It was then hand-rammed and the lift went down and came up again with the charge, which was slid into the chamber. The lift went down, the breech was closed, a firing lanyard clipped to the firing lock (if

The 9.2in Mark 9 mounting used a chain rammer instead of a telescoping type, seen here being tested before the gun shields were installed

No 3 gun, South Foreland Battery, Dover, camouflaged in March 1942

Front view of the 6-pr twin anti torpedo-boat gun

firing by percussion) or an electric lead plugged into the lock (if firing electrically), and the gun was ready. Down below the shield, the next shell was already waiting beneath the breech as was the next cartridge.

The Mark VI mounting was the same system, except that the gun had extra elevation, and the shell was trundled round on a narrow-gauge railway track laid on the floor of the pit. This model had been introduced in 1916, to offer a cheaper and easier method of moving the ammunition.

Mark VII provided power traverse and elevation, a power-driven rammer, a hydraulic wash-out (which could flush the gun chamber before opening the breech, to extinguish any smouldering residue of cartridge cloth), and an air-blast (which forced high pressure air into the gun immediately after firing, to disperse the cordite fumes from the muzzle before applying the wash-out and opening the breech). The simple shield of the earlier marks was replaced by a large rectangular gun-house; this mounting is easily recognized by the overhang at the rear of the gun-house roof, and the square-section box containing the rammer which protrudes behind the side of the gun-house.

These mountings were beautiful pieces of Victorian engineering; the complete gun and mounting weighed about 125 tons, and the gun could be revolved or elevated with no more than light hand pressure on the relevant control wheel. Power was provided from a central engine room through hydraulic mains laid underground; later, in some batteries, each gun had its own engine room, when it was belatedly appreciated that a lucky shot on the hydraulic main could disable all the guns. The engine rooms, whether central or individual, were always buried well underground and protected, while the magazines were even further down.

Drawbacks

The only drawback to these mountings was that they took a long time to manufacture and assemble, and required a good deal of highly specialized maintenance to keep working perfectly. In 1939, the Mark IX mounting, a simplified version of the Mark VII, was designed, to make manufacture easier. It is identifiable by its gun-house, which is closed at the rear end, with a door off to one side. The long-cased rammer was removed and replaced by a semi-rigid chain rammer, and the ammunition was brought up on a three-layered lift, which carried the shell and two half-charges. There were many other minor manufacturing changes, in the interest of easier production. Most of the many guns installed in South Africa, Australia, New Zealand and Canada from 1939 to 1945 were on Mark IX mountings; very few were installed in Britain.

Inside the twin six-pounder, when firing. The sergeant (right centre) is striking the firing lever of the right-hand gun, while the left-hand gun is being loaded. Note that he had a padded glove on his left hand for punching the cartridge into the breech. (The gun did not normally have such an array of senior NCOs; this was an instructor's course in training)

The Twin Six-Pounder

When, in the middle 1920s, the question of arming the proposed naval base at Singapore arose, it was apparent that entirely new armament would be required. The site of the new base, tucked away behind the island of Singapore, was a long way from the existing defences that had been built up over the years to defend the harbour. As far as the Royal Artillery was concerned, the problem was straightforward – the location and the potential threat soon dictated that the armament would require some very heavy guns, as well as some very fast-firing guns to deter small raiders.

The question of the fast-firing light guns had already been a matter of discussion – it was obvious that the 12-pounder was no longer good enough for this role and, by about 1924, the idea of a twin six-pounder was being examined. The design proceeded slowly while the political arguments about Singapore were being thrashed out; many of the drawing-office staff at Woolwich Arsenal had been laid off in post-war economy drives. At the same time, the heavier armament was decided upon. There would be 6in and 9.2in guns on 35-degree mountings, and, to deal with the heaviest potential threat, some 15in naval guns would be acquired, and provided with modern barbette mountings.

The process was delayed while the arguments between the Royal Air Force, the Royal Navy and the Army went on, periodically hindered by changes of government policy. Eventually, permission to go ahead with the rearmament was given and, in the mid-1930s, the guns finally began slowly to arrive. In fact, when Singapore fell, some of the guns had not arrived, and several of the 6in and 9.2in guns were still on 15-degree mountings instead of 35-degree ones.

One significant feature about the gun-mountings for Singapore was the fact that, with one or two notable exceptions, every one could make two complete revolutions to right or left of its zero position. The exceptions could not do so, not because of the mountings but because of the terrain; had they fired inland, they would have fired into a hillside. All the other guns not only could but did fire inland. Any defect lay in the fact that the government's penury had limited the supply of impact-fuzed high-explosive shells; the majority of the ammunition was anti-ship armour-piercing projectiles, not much use against foot soldiers walking through the jungle.

The twin 6-pounder, as it was always known, was officially called the '6-pounder of 10-cwt', to distinguish it from the 6-pounder anti-tank (7-cwt) or anti-aircraft (6-cwt) guns. The two guns were

One of the 15in guns of Wanstone Battery, Dover

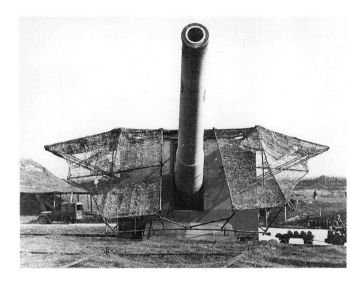

quite conventional weapons, with vertical sliding semi-automatic breech-blocks, set about three feet apart in the centre of a wide gun-house. Two gun-layers sat outside the guns, one aiming for line, the other for elevation, and the Number One had a control that allowed him to converge the left gun so that its shots struck in the same place as those of the right gun at whatever range was being engaged.

Behind the gun-house, which revolved on a pedestal mounting, was a curved concrete platform, around which a set of rails carried two trolleys laden with ammunition. Between the gun breeches and each trolley stood three men; the rear man picked a round from the trolley, passed it to the middle man, who grasped it by the base and swung it so that it came up under the arm of the front man. He seized it and thrust it into the breech, punching it home with a padded glove. The breech closed automatically, and, as the loader turned back to grab the next round, he slapped the firing lever on top of the breech and the gun fired. It recoiled about six inches, the breech flew open and ejected the spent case, and he had the next round in his hand ready to load. With two well-drilled lines, it was possible to get 120 rounds per minute out of a twin 6-pounder. Six of these equipments, in Fort St Elmo, Malta, blew an Italian human torpedo attack out of existence in about 90 seconds in July 1941. That

represents about 1,000 rounds of impact-fuzed high-explosive shells.

The 15in Gun, Marks I and II

The 15in was at the other end of the scale. The barrel alone weighed 100 tons and fired a 1,938lb (880kg) AP shell at 2,680ft/sec to a range of 42,000 yards (38,530m). No complete drawings of the mountings exist, but it is known that there were two types: the Mark I was more or less a scaled-up 9.2in barbette type of mounting; Mark II was closer to a naval turret, revolving on a huge roller ring, carried on a step in the concrete pit, and stretching some twenty feet down into the ground with its ammunition hoists and power supplies. There were the usual magazines, engine rooms, crew quarters and so forth, all underground, adjacent to the gun pits of both types of mounting. The Mark I gun mounting weighed 373 tons, and the Mark II, which had more machinery and armour, probably weighed half as much again.

Five guns and mountings, a mixture of Mark I and Mark II, were approved for Singapore; three went to Johore Battery and two to Buena Vista Battery, and all were mounted and operational by 1938. Two more were approved for Imbeah Battery on Blakan Mati island (now called Sentosa), but

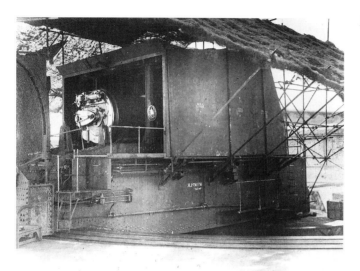

Breech end of a 15in gun at Dover

delays due to the sudden demands of rearmament meant that the fortress was taken by the Japanese before the guns could be shipped. They were, therefore, sent to Dover and became Wanstone Battery, built in September 1942. These two guns were on Mark III mountings, which appear to have been a simplified version of the Mark II, dispensing with the powered lifts and underground magazines, planting the roller race on a concrete foundation, and trolleying the ammunition in from magazines

build some distance behind the gun, and mounded over. The Singapore guns were cut up for scrap during and after the Japanese occupation, but the two guns at Wanstone remained in place until 1956.

The Dover Area

One last wartime innovation demands a mention: two batteries, each of three 8in guns, south-west of Dover. These were built in 1940 as part of a general

Averill Harriman, President Roosevelt's special envoy, inspects the 15in gun at Dover

A view of one of the Wanstone Battery 15in guns during the construction of the battery in 1942

thickening-up of the defences covering the Straits of Dover, to defend, and also to take aggressive action, against any German naval forces attempting to pass through the restricted waterway. Eight inches had not been a coast-defence calibre since 1907, when an earlier model of this calibre had been scrapped in favour of the 9.2in gun, but in 1940 anything that would shoot was acceptable. The Royal Navy had six surplus guns, which it offered to the Army.

The guns were provided with barbette mountings, modified from the standard naval pattern, and set into concrete pits. The Mark 8 guns fired a 256lb (116.12kg) AP shell at 2,725ft/sec to a maximum range of 29,200 yards (26,790m). Perhaps most remarkably, they were able to elevate to 70 degrees, a feature incorporated in the original naval mountings and retained in their conversion. This served no apparent purpose as far as sea bombardment was concerned, but when the V-1 flying bombs appeared over Dover in 1944, the guns were elevated and added to the general barrage fired into the sky. Whether they ever actually claimed a V-1 is uncertain, but a 256lb (116.12kg) AA shell-burst must have been an impressive sight. Although not strictly coast-defence artillery, mention should be made of two 14in guns mounted near Dover and manned by the 1st Royal Marine Siege Regiment. In the summer of 1940, Winston Churchill busied himself with improving the gun strength in the Dover area, in order to protect

convoys in the Straits of Dover and also, if possible, to deliver counter-battery fire against the heavy German guns being installed on the French coast. Vickers were given instructions to modify a proof mounting into a form of barbette mounting, and

Somebody has to take the muzzle cover off before firing. An 8in gun of Capel Battery, Dover, 1944

place a 14in Mark 7 gun on it. This became 'Winnie', and it was shortly followed by a second gun, which became known as 'Pooh'. Due to the mechanical limitations of the mountings, these guns were useless against moving targets such as shipping, but they did fire with some success against various German positions.

BRITISH RAILWAY ARTILLERY

Equipments and Their Locations

The British Army's railway artillery was made up entirely of leftovers from the First World War, some of which had not actually been completed when the war ended. The early extemporized models were scrapped, and only the most efficient of the later wartime designs were retained, scattered throughout military depots all over Britain and generally forgotten.

Lt-Col S.M. Cleeve, RA, who had commanded railway guns in France in 1918, was called upon by the War Office in November 1939 to form a Super-Heavy Railway Regiment. In a lecture to the RA Historical Society in 1982, he recalled his search around Britain for the remains of the railway guns. It was a fruitless task, until he reached the RAOC depot at Chilwell. Seeing 'an enormous and derelict transport shed away on the perimeter', he led the way there:

> With the greatest of difficulty, we forced the rusted doors open and gasped at what we saw. On the left

were Boche-Buster, Scene-Shifter and Gladiator [three WWI 14in guns], but none with any barrels. On the other two lines were about nineteen 9.2in Mark 13 guns and 12in howitzers, in a deplorable state, just as they were abandoned in 1919. Later, someone else found the mounting of Peacemaker [another 14in gun], but I cannot now remember how this came about. All were sent to various engineering firms to be refurbished.

Subsequently, a battery of two 9.2in guns went to France; the personnel managed to return via Dunkirk, but the guns had to be left behind. Three further batteries, each of two 9.2in guns and four 12in howitzers, were formed and sent to the Hull and Grimsby area as anti-invasion defences.

When Churchill turned his attention to the Dover area, the Admiralty offered three 13.5in barrels to the Army. Churchill ordered them to be assembled to the empty mountings of Gladiator, Scene-Shifter and Piecemaker (its name subtly changed from the WWI version), and handed over to 1 RM Siege Battery. At the same time, the construction of Wanstone Battery, with its two 15in guns, began. Finally, the 18in howitzer barrel (which had begun development in 1918 and was completed in 1919) was mounted on Boche-Buster, and parked near Canterbury in an anti-invasion role.

Elswick's Gun and Howitzer

The 9.2in Gun Mark 13 had been designed by the Elswick Ordnance Company, and was simply a double-bogie straight-back platform truck with an

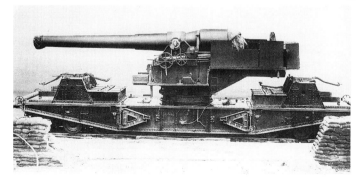

The British 9.2in Mark 13 railway gun

A 12in Mark 3 railway howitzer in France, 1939

improved Vavasseur mounting carried on a circular racer to give all-round traverse. A variety of guns were made available to fit this mounting (pulled together from various sources, but all fundamentally of the same calibre and length), and the maximum range was 22,600 yards (20,735m) with a 380lb (172.75kg) shell. The whole equipment weighed 87 tons.

The 12in Howitzer Mark 5 was another Elswick product, the third of a series of railway howitzers that were gradually improved. It was a relatively simple design, using a well-base double-bogie truck as a basis, with the gun mounted so that it could be

fired at any angle to the track. The aim was to provide 360 degrees of traverse, but it was simpler to give the howitzer 120 degrees of traverse either way, an amount that allowed fire at any desired practical angle. Outriggers could be fitted to stabilize the mounting when firing across the line of the track, and the maximum range was 14,350 yards (13,165m) with a 750lb (340kg) shell.

The 13.5in Guns

The 13.5in guns that the Admiralty offered to the Army in 1940 were from the reserve for the Iron

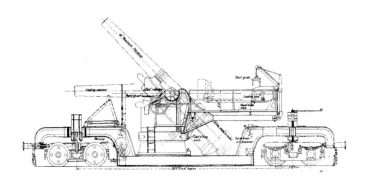

Handbook drawing of the 12in Mark 5 railway howitzer

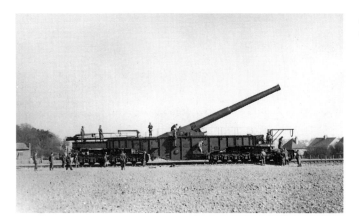

Preparing the 13.5in railway gun outside Dover in March 1943

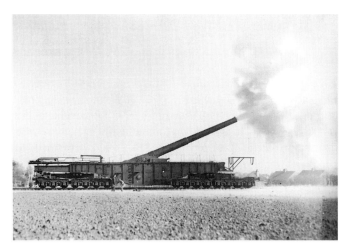

Piecemaker speaks; firing the 13.5in gun. If these two pictures were taken from the same spot, it is clear from the background that the entire mounting has recoiled several feet

The 18in howitzer fires from its railway cutting near Bekesbourne

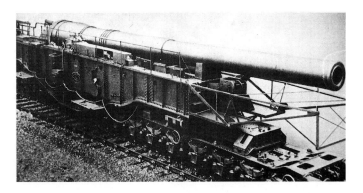

The 18in howitzer in travelling order. The metal framework is for camouflage netting for operational use, or for sheeting to disguise the shape while on the move

Duke class of battleships. They were close enough to the dimensions of the 14in guns used in the First World War to be able to be fitted to the same mountings, with a little adjustment here and there. The mountings were basically a steel box with trunnion mountings on the side plates, carried on four bogies, two four-axle at the front, and one four- and one three-axle at the rear end. A small amount of traverse was provided by attaching steel cables to the front end of the mounting, and using winches to pull it sideways across the bogie bolster; this allowed 2 degrees either side, which was sufficient to allow for fine adjustment. The initial coarse pointing was done by having a stretch of track on a 750-foot radius curve, along which the gun was pushed until it pointed in the general direction of the target. The brakes were then set, fine-laying was performed with the winches, and the gun then fired a 1,400lb (636.65kg) shell to a range of 32,500 yards (29,820m).

The gun was later provided with a 1,250lb (568kg) shell and a super charge, which increased the range to 40,000 yards (36,700m), and allowed cross-channel firing. And, contrary to old soldiers' stories, the gun did not recoil down to Dover and bring up the mail and rations on its return trip.

The 18in Howitzer

The 18in howitzer was in the course of construction when the First World War ended. It was conceived as a partner piece for the 14in guns, dimensioned so that it would be interchangeable on the same mountings. The howitzer was not completed until after the war ended, and was introduced into service some time in 1919. Four barrels were built, mounted, in turn, on one of the 14in equipments for test firing, and then dismounted again and placed in store. Later in the middle 1920s the 14in guns were sentenced obsolete and two 18in howitzers placed

The US 16in Mark 2 Mod I gun. Note the loading table and 'spanning tray' folded up behind the breech. Ammunition was delivered to the table by railway trucks and power-rammed across the spanning tray into the breech

An aerial view of a 16in gun Mark 2 Mod 1 on barbette carriage emplaced in the Panama Canal Zone

on mountings. Periodically one or other of these would rumble forth from its hiding place, to be deployed on Salisbury Plain, either on a siding near Bulford or at the terminus of the Larkhill Military Railway at Druid's Lodge, there to fire a few rounds into the range area. In 1938 one was taken to the Proof Establishment at Shoeburyness and removed from its mounting to be placed on a proof mounting and used for testing armour plate and other technical affairs; it is still there and rumour has it that there might even be one or two rounds of ammunition hidden away in a quiet corner of some magazine. The upshot of all this was that in 1939 there were four 14in mountings, one with an 18in howitzer on it

and three empty, and, as we have seen, these three were used to mount three 13.5in guns.

The 18in howitzer was mounted on Boche-Buster and spent its time on a railway siding at Bekesbourne, near Canterbury. It was frequently photographed with a variety of VIP visitors and was generally touted as a fearsome cross-channel monster, but the truth of the matter was that its maximum range with its 2,500lb (1,136.35kg) shell was 22,300 yards (20,460m) – barely sufficient to reach half-way across the Channel. Its only task was to bombard any landing beaches within its arc of fire, and since no landings were attempted it was never called upon.

Late in 1943 there was a move to assemble the

A 16in on Mount M4 and in a concrete casemate emplacement, typical of the wartime batteries erected on the west coast of the United States

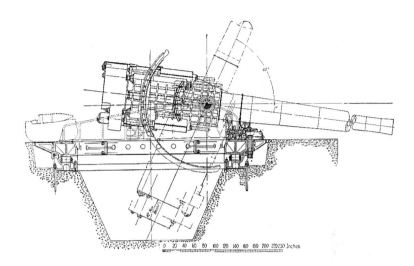

Drawing of the 16in Gun M1919 on barbette carriage M1919. This was generally the same as the later barbette carriages, differing only in minor details, and the drawing shows that quite a lot of excavation was necessary for these guns

three 13.5in (which the Royal Marines had finally handed over to the Army) and the 18in at Catterick and there form and train a Super-Heavy Railway Regiment to follow the invasion to France. An anti-concrete shell was developed for the 18in howitzer, and Boche-Buster was trundled down to Salisbury Plain once more to fire a few rounds in order to test them, but the idea was abandoned, the unit disbanded, and all the railway guns were withdrawn from their various coastal positions and placed in

store. They remained there until 1946, when they were wheeled off to the scrapyards.

USA COAST DEFENCE

Before the Second World War

As in Britain, the greater part of American coast-defence artillery dated from before 1914, and, provided that it was still capable of operating

Loading a 16in gun in Panama, 1942. The spanning tray had been lowered; the nose of the shell can just be seen behind the right-hand man. What the man with the long pole is doing is anybody's guess

efficiently and damaging an enemy warship, there was no good reason to replace it. Nor was there any money available to do so. The only relatively modern equipment was a score or so of 12in barbette guns, which had been developed in 1917 in order to achieve greater range than could be reached with the same guns on disappearing carriages.

The major counter-bombardment guns of the American defences had steadily increased in calibre throughout the years, from 10in in the 1880s, to 12in in the 1890s and 14in in the 1900s. However, as early as 1895, the Board of Ordnance was contemplating a further advance to 16in, and had developed a gun that was completed in 1902. It was used as a proof and test weapon for several years before work began on a disappearing carriage for it, by which time it was so worn that it had to go back to Watervliet Arsenal to be refurbished. Finally, in 1917, it was mounted at Fort Grant, Panama, where it languished, firing some twenty or thirty practice shots, until 1943, when it was scrapped.

These experiments had given the Ordnance Board and the Coast Artillery some ideas, and, in the enthusiasm of wartime, plans for another seven 16in guns on disappearing carriages were made. However, the size, cost and complexity of these carriages led to second thoughts; a barbette carriage was designed, which was not only simpler and cheaper, but also allowed the gun 65 degrees of elevation, ensuring that the maximum possible range could be achieved. In view of this, it seemed that there would be a chance to expand the 16in programme and install them in all sorts of places.

The US Navy was also interested in 16in guns for their forthcoming battleships, so a complete factory for the production of both guns and their ammunition was put together, and construction started. However, like so many of the 1917–18 American plans, the war ended before it could be half-started, and only the six guns originally intended for the disappearing mountings were made. The US Navy transferred their construction plans to existing arsenals, and settled down to a long wait for their guns.

The Washington Conference on Naval Limitation of 1922 scuttled the next generation of American battleships before they were even on the stocks, which left the US Navy with twenty completed 16in guns on their hands. They offered them to the Army for coast-defence purposes. Such windfalls were rare, and the Army authorities were happy to accept this one, even though they had little chance of mounting the guns for some years; although the new barbette mountings were relatively cheap, money was tight. They had managed to get six built for the 1917 guns, and had installed them in pairs outside New York, Boston and Pearl Harbor, but approval for a further six mountings was not obtained until 1924. Over the next ten years, these were built and installed in Panama and Hawaii.

Preparations for the Second World War

In 1938, approval was obtained to build six two-gun 16in batteries in the USA, and discussions began about the siting of more in the overseas possessions. The Navy produced another twenty-four guns from its stores and transferred them to the Army in the summer of 1939. In 1940, with the war looming closer, another twenty-four completed and forty-four partly completed guns were handed over. (One wonders by what sleight of hand the US Navy had managed to get finance for 112 guns for battleships that had been forbidden to them in 1922…) In the event, the building of the necessary mountings took time – other work had greater priority in 1941–44 – and, of thirty-eight projected two-gun 16in batteries, by 1945 twenty had been completed, and six were in course of construction. The remaining twelve were never begun.

The 16in Howitzer

The 16in howitzer was first thought of in 1917; if a 16in gun was to be made, then a howitzer of the same calibre was an obvious partner, given the American predilection for coast-defence mortars and high-angle fire. Each of the projected 16in gun batteries would be accompanied by a battery of

One of the four 16in howitzers at Fort Story. It differed from the gun only in barrel length and propelling charges; the barbette mounting was identical

Large numbers of 12in mortars were still in US service; here, a pre-war squad is being trained in loading

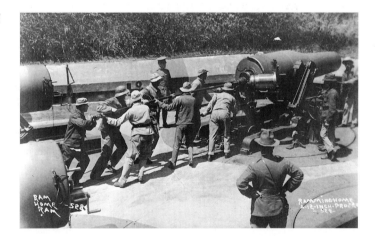

The 6in M1905A2 gun in Barbette Carriage T2, which was later standardized as the M2

howitzers. Manufacture of sixty howitzers was authorized, but the war ended before the project got into its stride, and only four were built. The mountings were slightly modified versions of the gun barbette mounting, and all four were sent to Fort Story, Virginia, to form two two-howitzer batteries covering the entrance to Chesapeake Bay. They were in place by 1922, and remained there until they were scrapped in the early 1950s.

6in Guns

The remaining armament of the coast artillery was, in the mid-1930s, exactly as it had been in 1918: a mixture of calibres, from 3in anti-torpedo-boat guns, 6-, 8-, 10-, 12- and 14in guns, mostly on disappearing carriages, and 12in mortars. In 1938 it became apparent that, in the event of war, there would be a demand for guns to defend naval bases and similar vulnerable points. The decision was

taken to construct a new well-shielded barbette carriage for 6in guns.

The elderly M1903 gun had been modified in the early 1930s to provide air-blast, in order to expel powder fumes before opening the breech. It was anticipated that, at some time in the future, it would have a shielded mounting that would require such an accessory, to prevent the fumes filling the gun-house when the breech was opened. This M1903A2 gun, and a similarly modified M1905A2, were now adapted to a new carriage. The Carriage, Barbette M1 had hydraulically power-operated elevation and traverse, and an all-round shield, while the M2 had electric power operation and was also fitted for remote power control from the Fire Direction Center.

The 8in Mark VI Mod 3A2

In 1940, it was felt that something heavier was needed in certain locations, and, since a number of

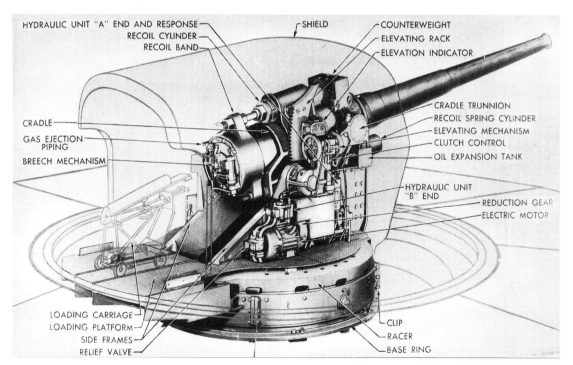

The 6in gun Barbette Carriage M2 with hydraulic power operation. The 'gas ejection piping' was an air blast to blow the fumes out of the barrel before opening the breech, to stop noxious fumes entering the gun-house

The 8in Mk VI Mod 3A2 on Barbette Carriage M1

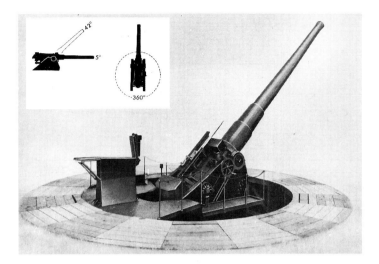

8in guns were being acquired for railway mounting, the number was increased, and a suitable barbette mounting was developed. This became the 8in Mark VI Mod 3A2 (the terminology reveals its naval origin), on Carriage, Barbette M1. This carriage was simply an enlarged version of the 6in M1 design, but without the power elevation and traverse and with a shield.

The 'Panama Mount'

In order to provide temporary coast-defence weapons, two expedients were developed. The first was the 'Panama Mount' for the standard 155mm M1918 field gun. This was simply a concrete pedestal with a pivot bolt, surrounded by a circular concrete ring. The gun was hauled into place so that its wheels sat on the central pedestal, where the axle was anchored to the pivot bolt. The trails were opened so that their ends rested on the concrete ring, and the gun could then be traversed fairly rapidly in any direction. Numbers of these emplacements were built in various places in continental USA and in the possessions, so that in the event of danger a nearby battery of 155mm guns could be quickly installed. Several were brought into use in 1941–42.

With the obsolescence of the M1918 gun, and the introduction of the M1, on a different carriage, it was necessary to revise the design. This led to the 'Kelly Mount', or 'Firing Platform M1', similar in principle, but differing in construction and dimensions, so as to suit the more modern carriage of the M1 gun. Relatively few of these seem to have been installed, principally on the west coast of the USA.

A 155mm M1918 gun on a Panama Mount, converting it into a passable coast-defence gun

183

The 90mm Gun M2

The second expedient was to adapt the 90mm AA gun to the coast-defence role, since it was a quick-firing gun with a good range and a destructive shell. The M2 gun on Mounting M2 had been designed so that it could be emplaced as a coast-defence gun and had sufficient depression to shoot down to sea level, but this was simply a side-line from its normal AA use. A purely coast design was needed, and this resulted in the 90mm Gun M2 on Mounting M3. The gun was in an armoured turret on a pedestal mount, but was still capable of 80 degrees elevation, so that it could still function in either the AA or the coast role. It was introduced in June 1943. A project for a slightly improved version, with heavier armour and slightly greater depression, was started at the same time, but a lessening of demand for fixed coast artillery became obvious in early 1944, and the project was cancelled.

USA RAILWAY ARTILLERY

Like Britain, America ended the First World War with a varied collection of railway guns, and a large number of building contracts under way. The contracts were cancelled immediately after the Armistice, but in one or two cases enough components had been made to allow several complete guns to be assembled. Since there was obviously more sense in that than in leaving piles of parts to rust away, the guns were completed and issued. The result was the issue in the early 1920s of thirty-seven 8in Guns M1888 on Railway Mount M1918, twelve 12in Guns M1895 on Mounting M1918, and ninety-one 12in howitzers M1890 on Mounting M1918.

The 8in Guns

The 8in guns were a mixed collection of Army and Navy weapons of different marks and models. The Army guns were 32 calibres long and differed only in minor details; the ex-Navy guns were of four types, varying from 32 to 45 calibres in length, and with four different types of breech mechanism. The mountings were simply rotating barbettes on well-base flatcars carried on two four-wheel bogies; they were built so that the standard-gauge bogies could be quickly removed and replaced with narrow-gauge (60cm) bogies, for use on the light railways laid behind the lines in France. This was later to prove useful to allow the guns to be moved around on sugar plantation railways in Hawaii.

With the pressure of war removed, the complications posed by the different styles of ex-Navy gun led to their being scrapped in the late

Gun, 8in, M1888 on Railway Car M1918; numbers of these survived to be deployed as coast-defence guns in 1941

The 8in gun Mark VI Mod 3A2 was also placed on to a railway mounting and deployed for coast defence

Handbook drawing of the 8in Mk VI Mod 3A2 mounting, showing the principal dimensions

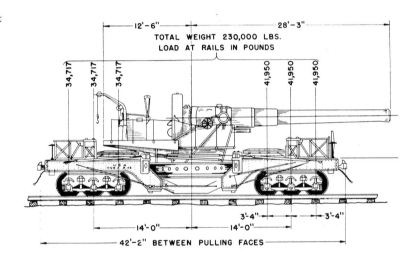

The 12in howitzer on railway mounting was another hold-over from 1918; many were deployed in the Philippines

1920s, leaving only the M1888 Army guns. Some of these were then removed from their flatcars and had the mountings set in concrete to provide additional coast-defence batteries, notably in Hawaii.

Back in 1918, the AEF in France had asked for a more powerful 8in railway gun, and plans were prepared for an entirely new 50-calibre gun and a new mounting. When the war ended, the idea was shelved. After the 1922 Washington Conference, the US Navy offered its surplus of 8in Mark VI 45-calibre guns to the Army. Recalling their wartime project, the Army was happy to accept these and set about designing a new mounting for them. In the interests of economy, the mounting for the 12in howitzer (*see* below) was adapted as the Mounting M1925E, a sample was manufactured and tested, and modifications were made. Then, in 1933, the money ran out and the project was cancelled.

In 1938, the idea was revived, and the modified M1925E became the Mounting M1. One was sent to Aberdeen Proving Ground, where it remained for the rest of its service. The design was simplified, becoming the Mounting M1A1, and it was finally standardized in June 1941. The final design was a well-base flatcar riding on two six-wheel Pullman bogies. The gun pedestal was in the well section, and the gun was fitted with a heavy counterweight, so that the trunnions could be set well back to allow plenty of room for recoil at maximum elevation. A loading platform extended behind the breech, and

loading was done at 5 degrees depression; the breech was opened and a 'spanning tray' placed between a loading table on the platform and the breech. The shell, on the loading table, was then pushed down the tray, gathering speed and assisted by a rammer, until it entered the chamber, and the driving band bit into the rifling. Eight outriggers steadied the mounting during firing, and jacks could be used to raise the car body, so as to insert firing supports between the body and the track, and thus relieve the suspension of any firing shock.

Twenty-nine of these guns were built, and a number were emplaced on the Pacific coast of the USA, particularly around Puget Sound and near Santa Monica. Not all of them were issued; several seem to have remained in store throughout their life. All were scrapped shortly after the war ended.

The 12in Guns and Howitzers

The 12in M1895 guns had been built by the Marion Steam Shovel Company in 1918–21, and appear to have trundled out of the factory and straight into store, where they stayed. One was used by the US Navy as a ballistic test gun, but it seems that the remainder were never issued for service. They were sentenced as 'Limited Standard' by 1941, and were scrapped before the war ended.

The 12in howitzers were treated more seriously and were more or less integrated into the permanent coast-defence system. Most were sent to the various

Demonstrating its versatility, the 12in M1918 howitzer fires across the track

The 14in Gun M1920 in firing mode (top), and travelling mode (below). Note how the top carriage has been lifted up to permit the gun to be fired and lowered to permit it to pass the railway loading gauge

coast-defence commands in the continental USA, including Delaware Bay, Chesapeake Bay, Mobile Bay and Puget Sound, where they were stored in convenient military bases. Suitable firing sites were reconnoitred, railway tracks were surveyed, some sites were graded and prepared for track, and a handful actually had track laid. The weapons were the standard 12in sea-coast mortar fitted into a top carriage, which revolved on the same well-base flatcar that carried the 8in gun. As with the gun mounting, the bogies could be removed and replaced by narrow-gauge units when necessary.

In 1941, these howitzers were rolled out of their bases, but many of them never went where they were intended to go; in many cases the track had never been laid, and the howitzers were diverted. In 1942, most of the howitzers trundled back into their storage yards and all but a handful were scrapped; those which escaped that time were scrapped in 1944.

The 14in M1920

The only major railway gun project which occupied the US Army in the inter-war years was the 14in M1920. This ambitious project aimed to provide a heavy support gun for the field army, and also a heavy coast-defence gun capable of being emplaced very rapidly wherever it was needed. The Army had probably been put on its mettle by the activities of

the US Navy in 1917–18; they had constructed five 14in guns and sent them to France, where they were active in support of the AEF while the Army was still talking about railway guns. The Baldwin Locomotive Works had built the Navy guns, and they went on to build another six for the Army, delivering them in 1919.

The Mounting

The Army was not particularly impressed with the Navy's design, so they dismantled the six weapons and rebuilt them into various experimental shapes. They tried out various mechanical ideas, and then set about designing a completely new equipment. The 14in Gun M1920 was a quite conventional 50-calibre weapon, which could fire a 1,208lb (550kg) HE shell to 48,200 yards (44,220m) range. The mounting was a girder structure carried on two sets of two bogies; the front pair had eight wheels each, the rear pair six wheels each. On top of this basic chassis went a 'top carriage', which was hinged to the basic structure at its rear end and carried the gun cradle at the front end. The rear axis was also on a pivot, to allow a small amount of traverse for fine laying, and the entire top carriage and gun could be lifted at its front end by two screw jacks. The object behind this complication was to have a travelling unit that would pass the standard railway loading gauge, but could then be lifted, to allow the breech sufficient room to give 50 degrees of elevation to

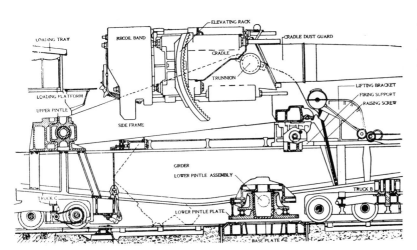

A drawing showing the details of the top-carriage lifting arrangement on the 14in M1920 railway gun

the gun, and allow the gun to recoil without striking the track bed.

Firing could be done either from the usual curved track or from a prepared emplacement. In the former case, the gun was pulled into position and steel girders were laid outside and parallel with the rails. The chassis was then lowered on its bogies until the body sides rested on the steel girders. Six outriggers were then installed, and the front end of the top carriage was lifted. This was done by electric power, the lift being some 170 tons, and six feet; there were hand cranks for emergencies (or, no doubt, for the chastisement of the truculent soldier). Once the top carriage had been lifted the full 74in, a 'firing beam' was run underneath by means of a rack-and-pinion mechanism, and the top carriage lowered on to it, taking the strain off the jacks. The gun could be ready to fire within an hour of arriving on site.

Emplacement

For its emplacement as a coast-defence gun, the procedure was more complicated. An emplacement had first to be built, using concrete and steel, and with a circular steel traversing track running around it. This, of course, was to be done during peacetime, as an insurance for the future. With the emplacement and a spur of railway line in place, the gun was run up the line until it was positioned above the steel baseplate. It was then lowered, until a 'pintle plate' beneath the carriage body engaged with the steel ground baseplate, and the two could be bolted together. The bogies were disconnected and trundled away, and a traversing roller unit, beneath the carriage body and 16 feet back from the pintle plate, was lowered, to ride on the circular traversing track. By operating a hand crank to turn the rollers, it was possible to traverse the whole 282 tons of carriage and gun around the ball-race set in the pintle plate, and a complete 360-degree rotation took about three minutes of cranking. From bringing the gun into place above the baseplate to having it ready to fire took about two and a half hours.

Delivery to Locations

This design became the Mounting M1920 and four were built. The first was the M1920M1, which had the breech of the gun canted to one side, to clear the recoil system; the rest were M1920M2, in which the gun was upright and the recoil system was modified to fit.

The first gun was despatched in 1927 across the USA by rail to Fort MacArthur, San Pedro, California, a journey that took an astonishing three months. It seems there was a succession of minor mishaps and breakdowns in the journey, most related to the running gear, including over-heated wheel bearings, sticking brakes, and similar nonsenses. All the defects were noted and steps were taken to see that they did not appear in the M2 models. The second gun was also sent to Fort MacArthur; the third and fourth guns were shipped to Panama, and were stabled at Fort Grant, at the Pacific Ocean end of the Panama Canal. All the guns were occasionally fired; the Fort MacArthur guns from Camp Pendleton, between Los Angeles and San Diego, and the Panama guns were moved via the Panama Railroad to Fort Randolph, at the Atlantic Ocean end, for their firing practice.

All four guns remained in these locations during the war. To camouflage the California guns, canvas imitation huts were built over them, and then similar, genuine, huts were built around them. If they were called upon to fire, a quick-release would 'split' the hut at the roof ridge, allowing the two halves to fall sideways to expose the guns.

As with the British guns, there was a proposal in 1944 to ship the M1920s to Europe as super-heavy support weapons, but the idea was quickly abandoned, and the four guns were scrapped shortly after the end of the war.

RUSSIAN RAILWAY ARTILLERY

Russian railway artillery appears to have begun in the days of the Tsar. In the early 1900s, a 10in (254mm) gun from an elderly battleship was put on to a railway mounting. The surviving pictures are so indistinct that it is impossible to determine any details of the equipment, although it appears to be a simple arrangement of a Vavasseur-type mounting on a flat-bed truck.

The TM-1-14

The next attempt began in early 1917, but was severely disrupted by the revolution. In the 1920s, the idea was revived, and the TM-1-14 came into existence. This was a 14in gun, again from an old battleship class, and the interesting thing about the design is the mounting. It is the usual girder box structure on double bogies, but, apart from a slight difference in the outline of the box, it is a virtual copy of the US M1920E gun, complete with its unusual top carriage, jacking system, and firing beam. It even has the same pivoting arrangement and traversing rollers for use in a prepared coast-

A 14in M1920 gun on its fixed emplacement in the Panama Canal zone

defence emplacement. The similarity of these two designs cannot possibly be a coincidence. The details of the M1920E were publicly discussed and illustrated in American engineering journals of the 1920–22 period, and these were surely assiduously read and copied in the Russian design office.

In the early 1930s, the design was repeated, this time using a 12in gun, but with exactly the same type of carriage, to produce the TM-1-12, followed by the TM-2-12 and TM-3-12, which used slightly different guns.

The TM-1-180

In about 1935, the TM-1-180, a completely different design from top to bottom, was developed. This used a 180mm naval gun, complete with its naval mounting and shield, placed on to a well-base flatcar on two eight-wheel bogies. Outriggers and rail clamps were provided to stabilize the gun, since it could traverse through 360 degrees. An intriguing feature of this equipment was a fixed circular platform, which surrounded the shielded gun; this was constructed in sections, carried on the mounting and assembled when the gun was emplaced, and surrounded by a waist-high railing. Extending from the front of this was a roller chute, connecting the platform with an ammunition rack on the front of the mounting. Attached to the platform railing were shell trays, so that ammunition could be pushed up the roller track and on to a tray, then trundled round the top of the railing to the gun breech and there hand-loaded. This must have been a lively pastime when the gun was firing.

Of the employment of these weapons little or nothing is known; one picture of the TM-1-12 shows it emplaced in a coast-defence role in some unidentified seaport, while pictures of the TM-1-14 give no indication of where or even when they were taken. A photograph of the TM-1-180 identifies it as being 'in the Moscow region', which suggests deployment in the defences some time in late 1941. However, the available evidence suggests that the number of railway guns in Russian employment was small – perhaps no more than 25 or 30 – and that their activities during the war were negligible.

Appendix: Data Tables

FIELD, INFANTRY AND MOUNTAIN

Britain

	Calibre (in)	Weight in action (lb)	Barrel length (in)	Elevation (degrees)	Traverse (degrees)	Recoil System	Shell Weight (lb)	Muzzle Velocity (ft/sec)	Max Range (yd)	Other Features
18/25pr Gun Mk I	3.45	3,096	97.0	30	4	HP	18.5	1,615	9,300	Improved version
25pr Gun Mk II	3.45	3,986	106	40	8	HP	25	1,700	13,400	
3.7in Mtn How	3.70	1,610	46.8	40	20	HP	20.0	973	5,900	Ultimate screw-gun
4.5in How	4.50	3,010	70.0	45	3	HS	35.0	1,010	7,300	
4.5in gun	4.50	12,880	185	45	60	HP	55	2,250	20,500	
60pr Gun Mk II	5.00	12,050	192.2	35	4	HP	60.0	2,130	15,550	Improved version

USA

	Calibre (in)	Weight in action (lb)	Barrel length (in)	Elevation (degrees)	Traverse (degrees)	Recoil System	Shell Weight (lb)	Muzzle Velocity (ft/sec)	Max Range (yd)	Other Features
75mm M1897	2.95	2,657	107.1	19	6	HP	14.7	1,955	13,950	French Mle 1897
75mm M1916	2.95	3,210	90.9	53	45	HP	14.7	1,900	12,490	
75mm M1917	2.95	2,990	88.2	16	8	HS	14.7	1,900	12,490	British 18pr
75mm How M8	2.05	1,339	52	45	6	HP	14.0	1260	9610	
105mm How M1	4.13	4,980	101.4	66	46	HP	33.0	1550	12205	
105mm How M3	4.13	2,495	68.2	69	46	HP	33.0	1020	8295	
4.5in Gun M1	4.50	1,2444	197.6	65	53	HP	55.0	2275	21125	

Russia

	Calibre (in)	Weight in action (lb)	Barrel length (in)	Elevation (degrees)	Traverse (degrees)	Recoil System	Shell Weight (lb)	Muzzle Velocity (ft/sec)	Max Range (yd)	Other Features
76mm M1902/30	76.2	1,350	3.05	37	5	HS	6.2	680	13,300	
76mm M1927	76.2	780	1.25	25	6	HP	6.2	387	8,550	
76mm M1933	76.2	1,600	3.85	43	5	HP	6.4	715	13,600	
76mm M1936	76.2	1,620	3.89	75	60	HP	6.4	705	13.600	

	Calibre (in)	Weight in action (lb)	Barrel length (in)	Elevation (degrees)	Traverse (degrees)	Recoil System	Shell Weight (lb)	Muzzle Velocity (ft/sec)	Max Range (yd)	Other Features
76mm Mtn M1909	76.2	625	2.94	28	5	HS	6.4	730	7,100	
76mm Mtn M1938	76.2	785	1.75	70	20	HP	6.0	495	7,000	
76mm M1939	76.2	1,485	3.20	45	60	HP	6.0	675	13,300	
76 mm M1941	76.2	110	3.25	18	27	HP	6.4	680	6,000	
76mm M39/42	76.2	1,600	3.20	45	57	HP	6.2	680	12,900	
76mm M1942	76.2	1,116	2.98	37	54	HP	6.2	680	12,900	
85mm M1943	85	1,705	4.68	40	30	HP	9.5	795	16,000	
85mm M1945	85	1,725	4.68	35	54	HP	9,5	795	15,500	
105mm Mtn M1909	105	730	1.10	60	5	HS	12	300	6,000	
107mm M1910/30	107	2,535	4.05	37	12	HS	17.2	670	16.250	
107mm M1940	107	3,957	4.65	44	60	HP	17.1	720	17,450	

MEDIUM/HEAVY ARTILLERY

Britain

	Calibre (in)	Weight in action (lb)	Barrel length (in)	Elevation (degrees)	Traverse (degrees)	Recoil System	Shell Weight (lb)	Muzzle Velocity (ft/sec)	Max Range (yd)	Other Features
5.5in gun	5.50	13,646	171.6	45	60	HP	100	1,675	16,200	18100 with 80lb shell
6in 26cwt How	6.00	8,144	87.5	45	4	HP	100.0	1,234	9,500	11400 yd with 86lb shell
6in Gun Mk XIX	6.00	10.15t	219.2	38	4	HP	100.0	2,350	18,750	
7.2in how Mks I-IV	7.20	22,760	171	45	8	HP	200	1,700	16,900	
7.2in How Mk VI	7.20	14.53t	248	63	60	HP	200	1,925	19,600	
9.2in How Mk II	9.2	16.25t	170	50	60	HP	290	1,600	13,935	Vickers
12in How Mk IV	12.0	37t	222	65	60	HP	750	1,468	14,350	Vickers

USA

	Calibre (in)	Weight in action (lb)	Barrel length (in)	Elevation (degrees)	Traverse (degrees)	Recoil System	Shell Weight (lb)	Muzzle Velocity (ft/sec)	Max Range (yd)	Other Features
155mm How M1917	6.10	8,184	91.4	42	6	HP	95	1,475	12,400	Ex-French
155mm How M1	6.10	11,966	122	63	49	HP	1,850	16,355		
155mm Gun M1917	6.10	25,905	234	35	60	HP	95	2,410	20,100	Ex-French
155mm Gun M1	6.10	30,600	290	63	60	HP	95	2,800	25,395	
8in How M1	8.00	31,700	209	65	60	HP	200	1,950	18,510	
8in Gun M1	8.00	30.93t	409.5	50	30	HP	240	2,840	39,635	
240mm How M1918	9.45	18.43t	204	60	20	HP	345	1,700	16,400	Ex-French
240mm How M1	9.45	28,88t	331	65	45	HP	360	2,300	25,225	

Russia

	Calibre (in)	Weight in action (lb)	Barrel length (in)	Elevation (degrees)	Traverse (degrees)	Recoil System	Shell Weight (lb)	Muzzle Velocity (ft/sec)	Max Range (yd)	Other Features
122mm M1931 (A-19)	122	7,100	5.64	45	56	Hp	25	800	20,850	
122mm M31/37	122	7,117	5.64	65	58	HP	25	800	20,850	
122mm How M1910/30	122	1,465	1.56	43	5	HS	21.7	364	8,940	
12mm How M09/37	122	1,450	1.71	43	4	HP	21.7	364	8,900	
122mm How M1938	122	890	2.80	63	50	HP	21.7	500	12,390	
152mm Gun 1910-30	152	6,700	4.26	37	9	HP	43.5	650	17,150	
152mm Gun M1910/34	152	7,100	4.92	45	58	HP	43.5	650	16,200	
152mm Gun M1935	152	18,200	7.00	60	8	HP	48.8	880	25,750	Model BR-2
152mm How M1909/30	152	2,725	2.16	41	11	HS	40	390	10,275	
152mm How M1910/30	152	2,580	1.67	40	9	HP	40	390	9,850	
152mm How M1938	152	4,150	3.75	65	50	HP	40	510	12,400	Model M-10
152mm How M1943	152	3,600	3.52	64	35	HP	40	510	12,400	Model D-1
152mm Gun/How M1934	152	7,100	4.40	45	58	Hp	43.6	655	17,600	
152mm Gun/How	1522	7,270	4.93	65	58	HP	43.4	655	17,410	Model ML-20
203mm How M1931	203	17.7tn	5.08	60	8	HP	98.5	61§0	18,000	Model B-4
210mm Gun M39/40	210	44.0tn	10.1	50	22	HP	133	800	29,360	Model BR-17
280mm How M1939	280	18.4tn					246	356	10,650	Model BR-5
305mm How M39/40	305	45.7tn	6.70	77	360	HP	330	530	16,580	Model BR-18

RAILWAY ARTILLERY

Britain

	Calibre (in)	Weight in action (lb)	Barrel length (in)	Elevation (degrees)	Traverse (degrees)	Recoil System	Shell Weight (lb)	Muzzle Velocity (ft/sec)	Max Range (yd)	Other Features
9.2in Gun Mk C	9.2	90t	442	30	360	C	380	2,700	21,00	Elswick
9.2in Gun Mk XIII	9.2	87t	335	40	360	C	380	2,100	22,600	Elswick
12in How Mk V	12.0	76t	225	45	240	C	750	1,468	14,360	Elswick
13.5in Gun Mk V	13.50	240t	626	40	4	C	1,250	2,550	40,000	
18in How Mk I	18.0	250t	648	40	4	C	2,500	1,880	22,300	Elswick

USA

	Calibre (in)	Weight in action (lb)	Barrel length (in)	Elevation (degrees)	Traverse (degrees)	Recoil System	Shell Weight (lb)	Muzzle Velocity (ft/sec)	Max Range (yd)	Other Features
8in M1918	8.0	70t	295	42	360	C	260	2,600	2,390	
12in Mortar M1890	12.0	79t	145	65	360	C	700	1,500	15,290	
14in M1920MII	14.0	325t	714	50	360	HP	1,200	3,000	48,220	

Russia

No details available.

COAST-DEFENCE ARTILLERY

Britain

	Calibre (in)	Weight in action (lb)	Barrel length (in)	Elevation (degrees)	Traverse (degrees)	Recoil System	Shell Weight (lb)	Muzzle Velocity (ft/sec)	Max Range (yd)	Other Features
6pr QF Twin	2.24	9.88t	109.7	7.5	360	HS	6.25	2,360	5,150	
12pr QF Mk I	3.0	4.1t	123.6	20	360	HS	12.5	2,258	8,000	
4.7in QF Mk V	4.7	8.7t	212	20	360	HS	4.5	2,350	16,500	
6in BL Mk VII	6.0	16t	279	20	360	HS	100	2,493	12,000	Central Pivot
6in BL Mk XXIV	6.0	25.4t	279	45	360	HP	100	2,825	24,500	
8in BL Mk VII	8.0	54t	413	70	160	HP	256	2,725	29,200	Dover only
9.2in BL Mk X	9.2	157t	445	15	360	HP	380	2,643	29,200	Barbette
15in BL Mk II	15.0	373t	650	45	240	HP	1,938	2,680	42,000	Dover & Singapore

USA

	Calibre (in)	Weight in action (lb)	Barrel length (in)	Elevation (degrees)	Traverse (degrees)	Recoil System	Shell Weight (lb)	Muzzle Velocity (ft/sec)	Max Range (yd)	Other Features
3in Gun M1903	3.0	9,290lb	175	16	360	HS	15	2,800	11,330	Pedestal mount
6in Gun M1900	6.0	50.5t	311	15	360	HG	105	2,750	16,500	Dis-appearing gun
8in Gun M1888	8.0	39.5t	278	18	360	HG	323	2,200	16,285	Barbette
10in Gun M1900	10.0	177t	420	12	170	HG	617	2,250	16,290	Dis-appearing
12in Mortar M1912	12.0	74t	201	65	360	HS	1,046	1,200	11,755	High angle
12in Gun M1900	12.0	300t	504	10	360	HG	1,070	2,250	17,345	Dis-appearing
12in Gun M1895	12.0	181t	443	35	360	HS	1,070	2,2509	27,600	Barbette
14in Gun M1907	14.0	284t	476	20	360	HG	1,660	2,350	22,800	Dis-appearing
14in Gun M1909	14.0	1,033t	560	15	360	HS	1,660	2,370	22,800	Turret (Fort Drum)

USA continued

	Calibre (in)	Weight in action (lb)	Barrel length (in)	Elevation (degrees)	Traverse (degrees)	Recoil System	Shell Weight (lb)	Muzzle Velocity (ft/sec)	Max Range (yd)	Other Features
16in Gun M1895	16.0	568t	590	20	170	HG	2,400	2,250	27,365	Dis-appearing
16in Gun M1919MII	16.0	484t	827	65	360	HP	22450	2,700	50,000	Barbette
16in Gun MkIIM1	16.0	433t	821	65	360	HP	2240	2,750	49,200	Barbette
16in How M1920	16.0	402t	432	65	360	HP	2100	1,950	24,500	

ANTI-AIRCRAFT ARTILLERY

Britain

	Calibre (in)	Weight in action (lb)	Barrel length (in)	Elevation (degrees)	Traverse (degrees)	Recoil System	Shell Weight (lb)	Muzzle Velocity (ft/sec)	Max Range (yd)	Other Features
40mm Mk1	1.57	4,368	117.7	90	360	HS	2.0	2,700	5,000	
6pr 6cwt Twin	2.244	11.0t	130.3	85	360	HS	6.0	3,100	21,000	
3in 20cwt Mk I	3.0	5.9t	140	90	360	HS	16.0	2,500	23,500	Towed, also truck
3.7in Mks I-III Mobile	3.7	9.17t	195	80	360	HP	28	2,600	32,000	Static weight 10.3t
3.7in Mk Vi	3.7	17.1t	252	80	360	HP	28	3,425	45,000	
4.5in Mk 2	4.45	14.75t	212	80	360	Hp	54	2,400	34,500	
5.25in Mk 1B	5.25	49.5t	275	70	360	HP	80	2,800	43,000	

USA

	Calibre (in)	Weight in action (lb)	Barrel length (in)	Elevation (degrees)	Traverse (degrees)	Recoil System	Shell Weight (lb)	Muzzle Velocity (ft/sec)	Max Range (yd)	Other Features
37mm	37	6,125	78.2	90	360	HS	1.34lb	2,600	10,500	Towed
40mm	40	5,549	88.5	90	360	HS	1.96lb	2,870	17,500	Towed
90mm M1	90	17,714	186	80	360	HP	23.4lb	2,700	34,000	
90mm M2	90	32,300	186	80	360	HP	23.4lb	2,700	34,000	
105mm M3	105	33,538	259	80	360	HS	32.7lb	2,800	37,00	Static
120mm M1	120	48,800	291	80	360	HP	50lb	3,100	47,400	Mobile

Russia

	Calibre (in)	Weight in action (lb)	Barrel length (in)	Elevation (degrees)	Traverse (degrees)	Recoil System	Shell Weight (lb)	Muzzle Velocity (ft/sec)	Max Range (yd)	Other Features
25mm M1940	25	1,073	2.29	85	360	HS	0.28	910	2,000	
37mm M1939	37	2,100	2.74	85	360	HS	0.73	880	3,000	
76mm M1931	86.2	3,650	3.37	82	360	HP	6.6	815	8,500	
76mm M1931/33	76.2	4,980	3.81	90	360	HP	6.6	800	8,500	
76mm M1938	76.2	4,300	3.88	82	360	HP	6.6	815	9,500	
85mm M1939	85	4,300	4.15	82	360	HP	9.2	880	10,500	

Russia continued

	Calibre (in)	Weight in action (lb)	Barrel length (in)	Elevation (degrees)	Traverse (degrees)	Recoil System	Shell Weight (lb)	Muzzle Velocity (ft/sec)	Max Range (yd)	Other Features
85mm M1944	85	3,850	4.69	82	360	HP	9,2	900	10,200	
105mm M1934	105	10.6t	6.30	80	360	HP	15	930	12,500	

ANTI-TANK ARTILLERY

Britain

	Calibre (in)	Weight in action (lb)	Barrel length (in)	Elevation (degrees)	Traverse (degrees)	Recoil System	Shell Weight (lb)	Muzzle Velocity (ft/sec)	Penetration	Other Features
2pr	1.57	1,757	82	23	360	HS	2.0	2,650	42/1000/30	
25mm Hotchkiss M37	25	684	75.8	26	37	HS	0.7lb	2,950	40/500/0°	
6pr	2.244	2,521	101	15	90	HS	6.0	2,693	74/1000/30	APDS = 146/1000/30
17pr	3.0	4,624	180	16.5	60	HP	16.7	2,900	109/1000/30	APDS = 231/1000/30
32pr	3.7	ca. 10t	195	20	50	HP	32.0	2,880	n/a	
3.45in RCL	3.45	75	68.5	Free	Free	Nil	11.0	600	n/a	Wall-buster shell
3.7in RCL	3.7	375	113	10	Free	Nil	22.5	1,000	n/a	Wall-buster shell

USA

	Calibre (in)	Weight in action (lb)	Barrel length (in)	Elevation (degrees)	Traverse (degrees)	Recoil System	Shell Weight (lb)	Muzzle Velocity (ft/sec)	Penetration	Other Features
37mm	1.45	912	82.5	15	60	HS	1.61	2,900	55/1000/0 APC	
57mm	2.244	28,101	117	15	90	HS	6.28	2,800	68/1000/0 APC	
3in M5	3.0	4,874	158	30	45	Hp	15.4	2,800	100/1000/0 APC	
76mm T3	3.0	4,190	163	15	60	HP	15.4	2,600	100/1000/0 APC	HVAP = 185/1000yd
90mm	3.54	6,800	186	21	60	Hp	17	3,350	122/1000/0 APC	HVAP = 255/1000/0
57mm RCL M18	2.244	491	61.6	65	360	Nil	2.7	1,217	65mm all ranges	HE range 4935
75mm RCL M20	2.95	165.5	82	65	360	Nil	14.4	990	200mm all ranges	HE range 6955

Russia

	Calibre (in)	Weight in action (lb)	Barrel length (in)	Elevation (degrees)	Traverse (degrees)	Recoil System	Shell Weight (lb)	Muzzle Velocity (ft/sec)	Pene-tration	Other Features
37mm M30	37	406	1.66	25	60	HP	0.8	762	36mm/ 500m/30°	
45mm M1932	45	510	2.07	25	60	HP	1.54	762	43mm/ 1000m/0°	
45mm M1942	45	620	3.10	25	60	HS	1.43	870	AP/HE; Max range 4550m	
							0.85	990	54mm/ 500m 30° HVAP	
57mm M1943	57	1250	3.94	25	56	HP	3.24	990	AP/HE; Max range 8400m	
							0.80	1180	100mm/ 500m/30° HVAP	
100mm M-44	100	3455	5.99	25	60	HP	15.88	895	APHE: Max range 20,650m	
							9.39	1100	181mm/ 500m/30° HVAP	

HP=hydro-pneumatic; HS=hydro-sprung; HG=hydro-gravity; C=combined (barrel rebuilds on carriage, carriage recoils on rails); S=sliding railway).

Glossary

When dealing with a subject as complex as artillery, using unfamiliar words, to describe various parts of the equipments or their use, is unavoidable. The following glossary provides all the necessary definitions in one place.

Airburst
The bursting of a high-explosive shell in the air above the target, which drives fragments downwards to attack personnel sheltering behind an obstacle or in trenches.

Asbury breech
A breech mechanism for bag-charge guns, which has a Welin screw (*see*), is rotated by a cam, and has a vertical operating handle on the right side. It permits opening the breech with a single movement of the lever.

Autofrettage
Method of manufacturing gun barrels by making the interior slightly smaller than the final required dimension, then injecting oil under very high pressure to stretch the metal to the required calibre. This places the inner portion of the barrel under compression from the outer and strengthens it.

Autosight
Form of gun sight used with coast-defence artillery. The sight is linked to the gun by a cam, so that, when the sight is aligned on the bow-wave of a ship target, the gun is automatically set at the correct elevation. It is based upon the triangle formed by the gun's height above sea-level, the horizontal range and the slant distance, and the

cam has to be specially cut for the individual gun.

Balancing gear
A method of counteracting the preponderance (*see*) of a gun by springs or other means, so that the elevating and depressing of the barrel can be easily done by a hand-wheel.

Barbette
A type of gun mounting allowing fire across a parapet but without cutting an aperture in the parapet.

BL (breech loading)
Term specifically used in British nomenclature to indicate a breech-loading gun firing bag charges and with obturation (*see*) performed by the breech mechanism

Bofors screw
Type of breech screw with the rear section parallel-sided and the front section conical, both sections having interrupted threads cut into them.

Box trail
A carriage trail with more or less parallel sides and a space between them, into which the breech of the gun can move in elevation and recoil.

Breech ring
Heavy steel block surrounding the breech end of the gun and enclosing the breech mechanism, not necessarily ring-shaped. It can also help to balance the preponderance (*see*), and act as a method of attaching the gun to the recoil system.

Buffer
That part of a recoil system which acts as a brake to the recoiling gun. Invariably a cylinder of oil, through which a piston head with a valve is pulled, so that the flow of oil through the valve acts as a restricting force.

Built-up gun
A gun constructed of a number of tubes or 'hoops', the innermost of which is the rifled portion. The others are successively larger and are shrunk on top of each other to reinforce the barrel.

Calibre
The internal diameter of a gun barrel measured across the lands (the raised portions between the rifling grooves). Alternatively, the diameter of a cylinder that will just pass through the gun barrel, in contact with the lands.

Chamber
The part of the gun barrel in which the cartridge explodes.

Chase
The part of the gun barrel in front of the trunnions.

Counterweight
A heavy metal casting attached to the gun in the region of the breech in order to counterbalance the preponderance (*see*). It may be designed into the gun originally or, more often, added in order to compensate for some modification – for example, the addition of the muzzle brake to the 25-pr gun demanded a counterweight on top of the breech.

Cradle
The part of the gun that supports the barrel and recoil system. May be a 'trough cradle', in which the recoil system is inside the cradle with the gun above it, or a 'ring cradle', in which case the gun passes through the cradle and the recoil system is attached above and/or below. The cradle usually carries the trunnions (*see*) and, with the gun, forms the 'elevating mass'.

Dead time
The time interval between setting a time fuze and firing it from an anti-aircraft gun. In the days of hand fuze-setting it was variable, depending upon the setter's skill and the agility of the loaders. The invention of loading and fuze-setting machines reduced it to a fixed value, and the arrival of proximity fuzes did away with it entirely.

Dial sight
Optical sight in the form of a periscope with rotating head, permitting the gunner to select an aiming mark in any direction for use in indirect fire. Also called 'Panoramic sight' or 'Goniometric sight'.

Direct fire
Artillery fire in which there is a direct line of sight between gun and target; as, for example, in anti-tank shooting.

Drift
The sideways movement of the shell during flight, which is due to the spin imparted by the rifling. For a given gun and projectile combination it is a constant value, which can be compensated for in the design of the sights.

Equilibrator
Another term for 'balancing gear' (*see*).

Firing jack
Alternative name for a firing pedestal (*see*).

Firing Lock
Attachment to the breech screw of a bag-charge gun into which a primer (*see*) is loaded in order to ignite the charge.

Firing mechanism
Attachment to the breech-block of a cased charge gun, which delivers either a blow or an electrical impulse to the primer in the cartridge case. May be inside the breech-block or attached externally.

Firing pedestal
A form of adjustable stand that can be lowered from the axle of a split-trail gun to give a single point of contact with the ground, and also relieve the wheels and tyres of the recoil shock.

Firing segments
Segment-shaped steel supports attached to the axle of a gun behind the wheels, so that they can be swung down and into contact with the ground to give firm support when firing.

Gun
Generally speaking, any artillery piece. More specifically, an artillery weapon firing fixed charges at elevations below 45 degrees.

Handspike
A metal or metal-shod lever used for lifting a gun or moving heavy equipment. Sometimes permanently attached, by a hinge, to the trail end.

Hangfire
An ignition failure in a gun cartridge, which results in a delay between pulling the firing lever and exploding the charge.

Howitzer
A gun that uses variable charges and fires at angles up to and above 45 degrees, so as to drop shells behind obstacles.

Hydro-pneumatic
Term used to describe recoil systems in which recoil is braked by a hydraulic buffer and the gun is then returned by a pneumatic recuperator (*see*). It is also used to describe equilibrators using oil and gas under pressure.

Hydro-spring
Term used to describe recoil systems using a hydraulic buffer and spring recuperator.

Indirect fire
Artillery fire in which the target and gun are not intervisible and which must, therefore, be controlled by a forward observer.

Jacket
A sleeve around all or part of a gun barrel, which supports the barrel and forms the attachment to the cradle or recoil system. It assists in giving longitudinal strength to the barrel to resist bending, but does not contribute to resisting internal pressure.

Jointed gun
A form of gun construction for mountain artillery, in which the breech and chamber section is separate from the chase and the two are joined by a screwed junction nut. Allows the carriage of a heavy barrel in two loads on mules.

Jump
Vertical movement of the gun barrel due to the shock of firing, which causes the axis of the bore to deviate from the angle at which the gun has been laid. It is a constant value for a given gun/projectile combination and can be compensated for in the design of the sights.

Limber
A wheeled carriage that can be attached to the trail end of a gun to support it for transport, thus converting a two-wheeled gun into a four-wheeled trailer. In light guns it may also be used as a means of carrying a small supply of ammunition for immediate use.

Liner
A tube, with chamber and rifling, inserted into a gun. It can be removed when worn and replaced, without the whole gun having to be dismantled. One way of changing the calibre of a gun is by reaming out the old rifling and inserting a liner.

Loading tray
A curved tray upon which a shell is placed and then presented to the breech of the gun, and from which it is rammed. May be carried to the gun by

hand, or may be a part of the gun's equipment attached by a hinge or crane device.

Misfire

Complete failure of a gun to fire when the firing lever is pulled. May be an ammunition defect or a mechanical defect in the firing mechanism.

Monobloc gun

Gun bored from a solid block of steel. The term was originally used to distinguish such guns from the built-up or wire-wound types, but is redundant today, since almost all guns are now monobloc autofrettaged type.

Mortar

Strictly speaking, any gun which fires only at elevation angles greater than 45 degrees. In practice, the term is now entirely confined to infantry mortars.

Muzzle brake

An attachment to the muzzle of a gun which deflects some of the emerging propellant gases sideways or slightly to the rear and thus generates a forward pull on the gun barrel. This reduces the rearward thrust of recoil and thus permits the firing of heavy charges without having to build an excessively heavy carriage.

Nordenfelt screw

Type of breech screw in which the breech ring is considerably larger than the barrel and is offset from the chamber mouth. The screw has a U-shaped cut-out on its circumference. When the breech is open, this cut-out is aligned with the chamber and the gun can be loaded. Rotating the breech screw moves the cut-out around and brings up a solid portion of the screw behind the chamber. Used on the French 75mm M1897 gun and its American derivatives.

Obturation

Term used to describe the sealing of the breech end of the gun against the unwanted escape of propellant gas. May be performed by a metal cartridge case or by a sealing device incorporated in the breech mechanism.

Pole trail

Form of gun trail that is a single strut of wood or metal immediately below the barrel, so that the amount of elevation available is restricted by the breech of the gun contacting the trail.

Predicted fire

Artillery fire in which the position of the gun and target are determined very accurately, and the range and azimuth calculated. These are then altered by corrections to compensate for wind, temperature, air density, differences in height , temperature of the propelling charge, shell weight and other variables, to produce a range and azimuth that will place the shell on the target without the need for an observer to make any further corrections.

Premature

The explosion or detonation of the projectile before it reaches the target. More particularly, the detonation of a shell inside the gun barrel due to some defect in ammunition or gun.

Preponderance

The imbalance of a gun barrel about its trunnions. If the trunnions were at the centre of balance, the gun would be easy to elevate and depress, but practical gun design demands the fitting of the trunnions closer to the breech, to leave room for the gun to recoil when elevated. This means there is more weight in front of the trunnions than behind them, and this excess of weight is the preponderance of the barrel. It is compensated for by the use of balancing gear.

QF (quick firing)

A British term used to indicate a gun using cartridge cases.

Recuperator

The part of a recoil system that returns the gun barrel to the firing position after recoil. It may be a bank of springs, compressed during the recoil movement, or a cylinder of compressed gas or air, further compressed during the recoil stroke. In either case, energy for the return movement is generated and stored.

Rifling

The helical grooves cut into the interior surface of the gun barrel in order to impart spin to the projectile and so stabilize its flight. Rifling may be 'uniform' – of the same pitch throughout the length of the gun – or 'increasing twist or 'progressive' – beginning at a slow pitch, so as not to impose a sudden torsional stress on the shell, but then gradually tightening the pitch as it approaches the muzzle. The amount of twist is specified either as one turn in so many calibres, or, in continental Europe, by the angle that the grooves make with the axis of the bore.

Semi-automatic breech

A breech mechanism in which the breech is opened by hand and, in so doing, a spring device is tensioned which, once the round of ammunition has been loaded, will close the breech automatically.

Spade

A blade-like fitting on the trail of the gun that digs into the ground and resists rearward movement due to recoil when firing

Top carriage

A component of a gun carriage that is above the wheels, supports the gun and cradle, and is capable of turning about a pivot, to permit traversing the gun from side to side.

Trunnion

Short cylindrical axles protruding from the side of a gun or cradle and resting in curved bearings in the carriage, allowing the gun to be elevated and depressed. The trunnions are retained in their bearings by 'capsquares'.

Vavasseur mount

A form of gun mounting, chiefly used in coast and naval guns, in which the gun was supported in a top carriage that slid up an inclined plane on the top of the mounting, the movement being controlled by two hydraulic buffers. After recoil, the gun ran down to the firing position under the action of gravity. It was later adapted to a number of railway gun mountings.

Vertex

The highest point reached by the shell during its flight. It can be roughly calculated by squaring the time of flight in seconds and multiplying the result by four; this gives the vertex in yards.

Welin screw

A type of breech screw in which the circumference is stepped in three diameters, two threaded and one plain. In conjunction with a similarly cut breech ring, it permits the screw to begin swinging open without requiring it to be completely withdrawn, so making the operation of the breech faster.

Wire-wound gun

A form of gun construction popular from about 1890 to 1930, in which the place of one of the barrel hoops (*see* Built-up gun) is taken by winding on miles of high-strength steel ribbon under tension. The resulting gun was strong, and lighter than a built-up gun, but deficient in longitudinal strength and liable to droop. It has been completely replaced by autofrettaged (*see*) construction.

Zone of the gun

A rectangle surrounding an aiming point, into which all the rounds fired by a gun set at the same azimuth and elevation for every shot will fall. The distribution of such rounds is governed by the usual probability laws, The 'fifty per cent zone' is that portion of this rectangle into which 50 per cent of the shells will fall, and this is tabulated in firing tables for every 100 yards of range.

Index